D1282706

I am a Composer

*

ARTHUR HONEGGER
at his home in Paris in 1954
photographed by A. Pfister

ARTHUR HONEGGER

I am a Composer

*

*Translated from the French
by Wilson O. Clough
in collaboration with
Allan Arthur Willman*

ST MARTIN'S PRESS
NEW YORK

Published in Great Britain
by Faber and Faber Limited
First published in United States 1966
Published in Canada by
The Macmillan Company of Canada Limited
Printed in Great Britain
All Rights Reserved
Library of Congress Catalog Card Number : 66-11638

JE SUIS COMPOSITEUR
was originally published
in the Collection 'Mon Métier'
('My Profession'), *Paris : Editions*
du Conquistador, 1951

TO HILDA GELIS-DIDOT

Translator's Note

*

This slender book, one of a series called *Mon Métier* ('My Profession'), though published in Paris in 1951, and translated into German (1952), Japanese (1953), Hebrew (Tel Aviv, 1954), Dutch (1956), and Hungarian (1960), has never before appeared in English. A parallel work by Charles Münch, entitled *I Am a Conductor* (Paris, 1954), was published in English (Oxford, 1955), as well as in Dutch, German and Russian. Yet Honegger's work would appear to possess no less charm and interest.

Arthur Honegger was born on March 10, 1892, in Le Havre, France, of Swiss Protestant parentage, and died on November 27, 1955. He studied music in Zürich and at the Paris Conservatory of Music, as he recounts in his autobiography, under such men as Capet (violin), Gédalge and d'Indy. After World War I he was one of the group known as *Les Six*, which included Milhaud and Poulenc, a group united by youth and a desire to challenge the musical establishment of the day.

Honegger lived chiefly in Paris from 1913 on. His dramatic oratorio, *King David* (1921), established his reputation. From that date on, his compositions ranged in number and scope far beyond our listing here. In 1923 came his *Pacific 231*, popularly assumed to be an interpretation of the modern locomotive, though he professed to see it as an exercise in gathering speed within a retarded tempo. Five symphonies, four of them composed after 1941, and a dramatic oratorio based on Paul Claudel's *Jeanne d'Arc au Bûcher* ('Joan of Arc at the Stake') (1934–1935), greatly enhanced his reputation as an artist of depth and power. His work further included compositions for the stage, theatre and film, and for choral and orchestral groups, as well as symphonies, quartets, and chamber music. Among the first type are scores for Shakespeare's *The Tempest*, Jean Cocteau's *Antigone* (1924–1927), and D'Annunzio's *Phaedra* (1923; Rome, 1926). The total list, indeed, would seem to challenge Honegger's pessimistic estimate of his own achievement. A study of Honegger's work was published in 1933 by W. Tappolet, but at a date too early to be comprehensive. A full list of his publications will be found in *Grove's Dictionary of Music and Musicians*, 5th edition.

M. Bernard Gavoty, his interrogator, though himself a student at the Paris Conservatory and an organist, is nevertheless best known as a music critic for *Figaro*, writing under the pseudonym of Clarendon. He is a Parisian, born in 1908, and, in addition to his work as a critic, is the author of several works on music.

The translation of this book was suggested to me by Mr. Allan Arthur Willman, chairman of the division of music at the University of Wyoming, himself a composer and pianist, who had long contemplated the translation, though other demands had intervened. During his studies in Paris Mr. Willman became acquainted with Honegger and other members of *Les Six*. I consented to undertake the translation on the condition that Mr. Willman would read critically the passages of a more purely technical and musical nature. His assistance in this respect has proved invaluable. He also prepared the music examples in Chapter 5. The final responsibility for the translation and the preparation of the text must, however, be my own.

The University of Wyoming   WILSON O. CLOUGH
Laramie, Wyoming
1965

Contents

*

CHAPTER 1

Letter to Bernard Gavoty
Pessimism Without
Paradoxes

*

Darkness, darkness . . .
   (*Joan of Arc at the Stake*)

My Dear Bernard Gavoty,

You ask me to submit a little volume on musical composition to the series entitled 'My Profession'. I do not wish to suspect the least bit of irony behind your proposal. I am to announce: 'I am a composer.' Imagine the listeners' smile if some gentleman should assert: 'I am a poet.'

Such a declaration, in the course of a police interrogation as to one's identity, would invite the proverbial rough handling. There are certain 'professions' which have to be labelled with a proper euphemism for our contemporaries, and which may not be associated with any but names of streets or tube stations.

Let us admit, however, that the 'composer of music' does still exist as a creator of sounds to be reproduced by the appropriate instruments. These sounds are suited to the soothing strings of an orchestra to be accompanied by the movement of two persons performing in a restricted space under the impression that they are abandoning themselves to the choreographic art. They may also furnish a rhythm for the experiences of a couple more or less well matched who must conquer a thousand obstacles before they can embrace in complete good conscience. When photographed, this is known as the cinema, or when played in 'flesh and blood', it becomes the lyric theatre or the operetta.

The above formula does indeed constitute a profession which may happen to be lucrative. For others it is a gentle monomania, a harmless weakness of which only a few know the existence. Nevertheless, a too considerable number of young folk are seized by it; and neither age nor experience will produce a cure for it.

It is in this last category that I must include myself, though in my case retaining a certain lucidity, which, I suppose, is your excuse for asking this little book of me.

This explanation, added to the too exclusively peevish remarks that I allowed myself in one of our radio interviews, will be the base from which I consent to attempt to say what I think—at least in part.

It is likely that for a period of time, the extent of which I, being no prophet, cannot determine, a small group will persist in producing musical scores; and another will sometimes come to hear them. But they will attract less and less attention. I shall develop this proposition in detail. I sincerely believe that a few years hence the musical art as we conceive it will no longer exist. Like the other arts, it will disappear, though no doubt more speedily. We already see what is happening in our day; let us look at the evidence. No one any longer listens to 'music'; they come to view the performance of a famous conductor or a celebrated pianist. And that, as we know, comes nearer the domain of sport than of art.

This point of view we shall develop later. Without infringing on the realm of the other fine arts, we have but to glance, for example, at painting, and observe to what monstrosities it is condemned if it hopes to command attention.

*

I believe it was Léon Daudet who first mentioned the 'stupid nineteenth century'. Is it responsible for the dizzy avalanche of the twentieth toward the abyss? Possibly. Nevertheless, it was that century which gave to France, to cite no other country, its very greatest musicians: Berlioz, Debussy, Fauré, and twenty more: poets like Victor Hugo, Verlaine, Baudelaire, Mallarmé, and others; writers in abundance; and finally, a school of painting and sculpture without equal. Further, civilized countries then knew a peacefulness that has since been banished. A man was permitted to have a few francs in his pocket without the State's intervention to take them from him; or better still, making him pay in advance what he might hope to earn. He could carry them from one country to another without accumulating authorizations, permissions, fingerprints, passports of all kinds, and more; all of which we hold to be proofs of the crudest barbarity. Since then, wars have succeeded wars, always in the name of 'Justice and Liberty', but in actuality resulting in the banishment of this liberty almost entirely from the face of the globe. All these exertions converge toward a single goal: a definitive war, which will liquidate everything. The most obscure minister of finance in free democracies wields today a heavier tyranny than that of the Roman Caesars. The Treasury is a despotic master before whom all must bow. 'Social Progress' regiments each one of us into the life of a concentration camp, making it all but impossible to survive as an independent being. The scholar and scientist are enrolled under directive powers. The 'benefactors of humanity' are outmoded by events, and no longer accept responsibility for the destructive machine which they have set in motion, and from which they have leaped in haste, confident of their own impunity.

A country must furnish billions to stretch an iron wire to block the path of this instrument of extermination launched at top speed against another. All are labouring for the annihilation of a civilization, to be touched off by a destructive machine. What will remain for art and music? When our two mechanisms have pulverized each other, when all sorts of bombs have turned the world into a heap of rubbish, a few survivors will no doubt be found amid the ruins of prostrate cities and scarred fields, seeking some subsistence. Then the ghost of a civilization will be slowly reborn, though we shall most likely not see it prosper.

Do you really believe that a creative genius, which is to say, of the type 'individualist', could in such case long maintain the possibility of survival, of devoting himself to his art, and of writing music? The first concern would of necessity be to avoid perishing from hunger and cold. Such is the future I envisage— and all too near at hand.

I sketch this future without the slightest pretence of prophesying in political matters. I am the man in the street. I simply state that the act of devoting oneself to the art of music does not demand that one delude oneself as to the future, or take refuge in an ivory tower. This is not a personal recrimination which I try to express: it is a focal point from which I hope to render some service to a future generation, to arm it with patience and courage.

*

Let us write, then, with serenity on the profession of being a composer of music, as if this future lay reasonably before us, full of happy promise. Nevertheless, I prefer not to draft these pages alone, with the pessimism of an old man's rule, knowing that youth will want to find reasons herein for hope in a possible future.

Therefore I propose, my dear Bernard Gavoty, to employ the form of the dialogue, as Gide did for his *Corydon*, and many others before him. Whenever my too bitter inferences shall seem to you to exceed the limits, a caustic glance from your clear eyes will suffice to check me, and your insights will oppose me with arguments which I shall be only to happy to accept; for I have children who may reasonably hope to live even to the year 2000!

Arthur Honegger

CHAPTER 2

Complaints

*

It would be interesting to know what
decides a man to become a paper-
manufacturer instead of a baker. . . .

HONORÉ DE BALZAC

ARTHUR HONEGGER: The profession of composer of music offers
the peculiarity of being the activity and the preoccupation of a
man who exerts himself to manufacture a product which no one
is eager to consume. I might even compare it to the manufacture
of top hats, button shoes and whalebone corsets.

We know well enough how little the public of today cares for
these objects which only yesterday were the signs of a most
refined taste. In music, though here my comparison breaks
down, everyone wants only what was manufactured a hundred
years ago. For this public, the art of music is summed up in the
performance of classical or romantic works. The contemporary
composer is therefore a sort of intruder who persists in stubbornly
trying to impose himself at a banquet to which he has not been
invited.

BERNARD GAVOTY: People are sincere when they express so
absurd an opinion; they are convinced that genius is an attribute
of centuries past.

A H. It is clear that the first specification for a composer is to be dead.

B G. Genius– that posthumous decoration–

A H. The listener swallows what is put before him with appetite or with disgust, but he is interested only in what he is made to hear frequently. That is why new works arouse a distrust which is translated into staying away from 'first performances'.

B G. The more one hears a great work, the greater the desire to hear it. That is a fact of experience.

A H. The question is not solely, as the critics think, one of 'modernism' being played, but one of opportunities to hear. For example, Ravel cannot be considered a 'classic' composer in the public sense, for he is heard. He wrote *Daphnis and Chloe* in 1912. This work had not been very often played for some thirty years. Suddenly, after a particularly brilliant performance given by Charles Münch with the Concert Society of the Conservatory, it caught on. Since then, the Second Suite of *Daphnis* is played quite regularly. I have seen it advertised five times in the same week. All at once it made its way into that restricted domain of 'works which are played'; thus it might appear with a Beethoven symphony or the Overture to *Tannhäuser*, because every orchestral conductor can announce it without risk.

Another characteristic example: that of Brahms. No one in France wanted to hear him. The critics jeered at his Teutonic heaviness, his immoderate verbiage, etc. But certain famous foreign conductors progressively imposed him. Today he is admitted to the same rank as Beethoven or Berlioz.

B G. Let us return, if you will permit, to this comparison between the artist of the past and today's composer. The classical musician found lodging with a Maecenas and enjoyed frequent commissions.

A H. It is obvious that the composer is no longer what he once was: performer, pianist, organist, violinist. Having mastered the rules of composition, he wrote to replenish his repertory. In those days—and we must emphasize this great difference—the listeners demanded new works! So it was for Haydn, Telemann, Handel, and many others. This explains the abundance of their output. They were solely artisans creating according to the established canons. Many of their scores so resembled each other as to make it difficult to distinguish one from another. Whether sonata or symphony, one served as a model for another. Generally, an opening theme, based on the notes of the principal key. A second in the dominant or the relative major; a coda leading to the double bar, such as is still found in Beethoven. The exposition was replayed to give the listeners full opportunity to become familiar with the themes. Next came the section called development, sketched as a fugal divertissement; the listener was given fragments of the first motif on harmonic progressions, followed by a pedal which reintroduced the principal key. After that, the exposition was quite simply repeated, and the whole was concluded with a reaffirmation of the original key; and the first part was completed.

BG. Fortunately, that did not prevent Haydn or contemporaries like him from having an original idea from time to time, a kind of good fortune of the pen which was the mark of their genius.

AH. That is why some of them became the great masters. Others, who did the same labour as artisans, have left no trace. But they comprise an inexhaustible mine for musicographers who periodically inflate them.

BG. A hundred and fifty unpublished quintets of Boccherini were recently uncovered. The number of his productions was already considerable; nevertheless, here, in one stroke, were one hundred and fifty new numbers for an opus. You can well imagine how the gourmets will swoop down upon them, licking their lips and proclaiming that these quintets are individually unique. The musicologists will have a fine time proving that this one is firmly classical, and that one contains already all the secrets of romanticism.

A H . Just the same, people will go to hear them for the perfection of their performance much more than from curiosity as to the the works themselves.

B G . The public, thoroughly indoctrinated, will see in them what the specialists have already decreed for them. If they are told that Boccherini never ceased to revitalize his style, they will believe it.

A H . Such is the critic's accountability! If a modern composer rates himself as a thinker or a philosopher, if his dream is to revolutionize the art of music with each new score, it is because he is driven to it by the music critic who decrees: 'This brings nothing new.' How often have I heard this verdict! I recall an imbecile who wrote disdainfully, after hearing Debussy's *La Mer*: 'Cocteau is right [though I am convinced that Cocteau never said anything of the sort]: it is a quite useless extension of *Pelléas*.'

B G . The naive misconception of the layman is that a great artist can and must forever be modifying his talent.

A H . At the same time, the public loves to recognize in a comedian what it has enjoyed before. In the realm of the song, the public always clamours for the 'famous' song of the film star that it has already heard on recording or radio.

B G . The public does not know what it wants. If we may shift to the loftier level of 'great' music, consider those who applauded Arthur Honegger, author of *King David*, and who yet demand of him on top of this a quite contradictory manifestation: that he remain faithful once and for all to the style with which he is identified, and yet at the same time evolve. This is like asking a horseman at full gallop to remain perfectly motionless.

A H . Let us not concern ourselves with the public more than is utterly necessary. But let us deplore its laziness. Here it is no longer the contemporary author speaking; it is the musician defending his predecessors as well as his peers and his juniors, and regretting the narrowness of taste. Beethoven is the god of

the enthusiastic music lover; so be it. But this does not prove
that his work as a whole is equally admired. Among his symphonies–

BG. There are the 'noble' and the 'less noble'. The noble are
those with sub-titles: the *Eroica*, the *Pastoral*.

AH. We touch on the great tragedy of our age: the more numerous the concerts, the less is music understood. The work is
only the tightrope stretched for the acrobat, orchestral leader or
pianist, and since there are inevitably certain works resifted to
the point of weariness, the repertory shrinks instead of growing.

BG. Such is the singularity of music. For it is not the same in
painting or literature.

AH. I am frequently astonished that the same public which
clamours for novelty in literature or painting–however horrible
it be–which is so eager to profit by every new invention, from
aviation to television, from cortisone to the hydrogen bomb,
remains so immovable and unresponsive in the single domain of
music.

   In literature, in the theatre, it is not the classics alone that
arouse enthusiasm. People go to see a play by Molière if Jouvet
has designed the stage setting; that's what counts. But they
prefer a new play by Anouilh to one by Racine, or, on a lower
level, a vaudeville by Jean de Létraz. They understand these
writers better than they do the classics; for they speak the
language of today. But in music they want a language dating
back at least a hundred years. Young people read Sartre, and
neglect Victor Hugo, Chateaubriand and Zola. They rush to the
new films, no matter how mediocre. Every year, the Prix Gon-
court assures a vast public for its winner–even if his name is
unknown.

BG. If Jean-Paul Sartre has more readers than Stravinsky has
listeners, is it not because the rapid evolution of musical language
frightens off those who cannot follow it? Confronted by a new
work, the everlasting refrain is: 'We cannot like that; we can't

even judge it. It grates on our ears, and your alleged pleasure is only frightful torture.'

A H. The critics say such things much more than the public. In Walt Disney's film *Fantasia*, no viewer was shocked at hearing the *Sacre du Printemps*, which they could listen to between the *Pastoral* and a ballet by Ponchielli. But the *Sacre* aroused indignation in many people at concerts. The eye always takes precedence over the ear. Actually, people don't listen! In my opinion, the work which is clearly developed, which follows a perceptible progession, planned by a conscious act of will, almost always finds the ear of the public, whatever be the harmonic and contrapuntal content of its composition. A certain roughness no longer shocks anyone, after what we have heard in recent years. The real danger is the boredom which is a consequence of so many clumsy improvisations. But, above all, there must be frequent opportunities to hear those works which may frighten at first contact. The audience manages to assimilate them quickly enough when they are viable. Look at Ravel!

B G. All the same, a new symphony is a bitter pill; it has to be sugar-coated to be swallowed. A renowned virtuoso, a famous conductor, is quite willing to play the role of sweetener.

A H. Nevertheless, the 'snob' element of the public demands extremes, in order to be fully assured of the novelty of the work. The confusion between daring and incompetence is constant. 'You don't like this work,' they say mockingly; 'yes–such things are a bit rough; to understand them, you must have studied.' 'No, Madame, I understand them only too well, but I see that it is a wretched job. The outward formlessness masks the absence of real invention, of genuine daring.'

These same credulous folk go into transports, and mistake for rare novelty what are but harmless imitations of drawing-room composers. When a Satie makes a pastiche of Chaminade or Hedwig Chrétien, they cry genius. Reaction against Debussy, Strauss? Doubtless, but above all, ignorance of music as such.

'A collaborator with Cocteau and Picasso can only be an avant-garde musician,' says the fashionable concert-going public; 'and besides, he is all the rage in the best dressmakers' shops.'

BG. Between the avante-garde and the rearguard, does the public ever actually discover a work to its own taste?

AH. Following the performance of one of my scores a gentleman said to me: 'It's very fine, but–it's strange–I thought you wrote modern music! Basically, it is as classical as can be.' Nevertheless, without any aggressive choosing of sides, my work was quite the opposite of classical. But the good fellow, not having been shocked, concluded that mine was the vocabulary of a Beethoven. Flattering comparison!

BG. Poor public, so often duped! What disgusts it with modern music is bad modern music. Ninety-nine impossible concertos deliver the fatal blow to the hundredth, which is excellent.

AH. You are right, up to a point, to defend the great public. They do not grasp the rules of the 'snob' game. They react by a convention which is not easily sloughed off. They lack the curiosity and the desire to hear new works. I often share their feeling. I have participated in concerts of modern music from which I emerged saying, 'If I had had to pay for my seat, I should have been bitter indeed.'

BG. You see–

AH. The really guilty ones are the critics. They too often lack a sense of proportion and of relative values. With the praise-worthy intention of helping youth, they apply the same laudatory terms to the work of a true composer and to formless lucubrations.

BG. It's a question of language. No one is deceived by it. The reader grasps very well the nuance which separates hackneyed praise of an unfortunate author from the victorious notice which salutes success. But it is not for me to instruct an old critic like you!

*

AH. You were right in saying that of a hundred scores, at least ninety-nine prejudice the cause of contemporary music. But the public, which can show its appreciation of a book, a canvas, a piece of sculpture, cannot do the same for a musical production until it has heard it. Without that hearing, the greatest masterpiece is for most amateurs nothing but sheets of paper covered with indecipherable marks. That is the curse that hangs over our art. Books are easily marketed; a canvas or a statue can be viewed for a modest fee; but the performance of a score requires a very substantial investment.

BG. These practical considerations weigh heavily on music. Nevertheless, a masterpiece always makes itself felt in the end. Come, let us pump up our optimism—and especially yours, mon cher Maître. Was there not spontaneous approval of your *Joan of Arc at the Stake*? For once, the layman was united with the professional to acclaim as one the birth of a masterpiece. However thick the fog, a lighthouse will always rally the drifting ships.

AH. The comparison is flattering, but it scarcely convinces me. You want me to be cheerful at all costs—that is to say, in a state of naive wonderment.

BG. I find myself confronted with a double paradox. A famous and honoured artist looks with a quite discouraged eye on the future of his art, and passes a sceptical judgment on a civilization in which music holds a very considerable place. Let us not be pessimists on principle!

AH. There are, indeed, a great many concerts and musical exhibitions, attracting a much greater public now than in 1900; but, I repeat, less new music is actually played today than formerly. Once more, nine-tenths of these demonstrations are closer to the virtuosity of sport.

As for my 'success', I attribute it to the fact that my career began in a climate the exact opposite of our present one, following the armistice of 1918, in an era when a general feeling of well-being prevailed. We believed that a new war was impossible, that the world's energies were moving towards science, art, beauty. Young composers, such as my comrades and I, found all doors open. We had a thousand advantages which the youth of today cannot imagine, and which I shall not even enumerate, lest I seem to denigrate them. Imagine that at twenty-two, after having written some small pieces of no importance, one might be offered a yearly contract by publishing houses; but today, composers with a reputation, whose biographies have been written, cannot find a way to publish their works. Editors are crushed by such practical burdens that they cannot publish the symphonic works of new composers without committing themselves to a veritable system of subsidization. We shall speak of that later.

BG. Still, your pessimism is quite relative. That our era is one of a host of difficulties is, alas, undeniable!

AH. I shall go further: I believe that we are living in the last stages of our civilization; inevitably, these last moments are painful. They will be more and more so.

BG. Are you alluding to the hypothetical annihilation of the globe, or simply of a world with no further room for the expressions of art?

AH. The two are inseparable.

BG. True, the end of the world would automatically involve the end of music. The reverse is not so certain. And for the moment, musical life is flourishing enough.

AH. Yes and no. Once again, on the score of quantity, the volume of music, you are right. And yet, see how the repertory of pieces performed shrinks. You will admit that they are already beginning to choose among the symphonies of Beethoven. If such selection is in operation on the work of the most performed composer in the world, how can you expect the situation to improve for second-rate authors, especially for young men whose work is still unknown? It can only become increasingly serious: for the repertory will not be replenished by virtue of the decline we are now experiencing.

BG. Well then, what future for music do you foresee in this lugubrious universe of yours?

AH. You know that a man exposed continuously to a powerful light finally grows blind. Our existence is increasingly dominated by the noise amid which we live. By force of living in such noise, we shall in a brief time be quite deaf. Your landlady's radio or your neighbour's pours forth a flood of noise from dawn to midnight. It might be the Mass in B minor or the vile belchings of lunatic accordions. You hear it everywhere, in the streets, in the shops, cafés, restaurants, even the taxis. It is even forced on one in the factories. Do you persuade yourself that a man who has heard the Symphony in C minor perhaps six times in one day is going to rush to the concert hall in the evening to pay a relatively high fee to hear it a seventh time? Many school children and students do their mathematics homework in front of their radio set in action. They become accustomed to thinking of music as a 'noise in the background' to which the mind pays no attention, no more than to the whitewash on the wall. Would we look at a Velazquez endlessly repeated before our eyes? That is what is ahead in the near future.

As for the present? They say: The public does not want to hear this, that. But perhaps the public, on the contrary, would like to hear this oftener than that. Only, who determines what will be performed? Look at the notices of the lyric theatre. In fifty years the repertories of the Opéra and the Opéra-Comique have hardly changed. Let some new director appear, and he announces to the press: 'I am firmly resolved to introduce all the newest things into this theatre, etc., etc., and to revitalize the repertory.' It is as convincing as a politician's speech at the conclusion of a banquet, for right away they replay the set pieces which draw the crowd. I was told one day at the Opéra-Comique, 'Actually, if they want things to go well, they should play *Carmen* every evening.' The public is composed of old folk: they don't want to hear anything but the successes. They go to hear *Manon* to recapture the emotions of their youth. The old gentleman comes with his wife, and when they come to 'Farewell, our little table,' he presses her hand and says, 'Do you remember, when we were engaged?' If he were forced to listen to Alban Berg's *Wozzeck*, his dignity would be wounded. The chasm that has been dug is so wide that, in all good faith, the public cannot be interested in the modern theatre.

Before the events which we owe to the initiative of certain clever leaders of the people, two countries still took the lyric theatre seriously–Germany and Italy. But there, too, all is slowly rotting. In Italy, most of the ruined concert halls are replaced by the cinema or garages. The theatre is an abyss from the point of view of financial investment. It is allowed to fall into ruin; the garage is such good business! Recently in the news-bulletin from Vienna, *Für Wirtschaft und Politik* ('For Domestic Economy and Political Policy'), Dr Nemetz-Fiedler stated that during the last thirty years very few works had penetrated into the repertory. The fact is, he surmises, that the lyric work is the expression of a human suffering lost in an age when the human being is increasingly swallowed in the anonymous mass.

I pass now to the realm of the symphony concert. The symphony concert is directed by committees which determine the programmes for the year. What happens? To open the season, they decree a nice little cycle of Beethoven. So they play the symphonies of Beethoven. After that, they reproduce almost literally the programmes of preceding years. Orchestral leaders are content: it means less work; and the musicians are delighted, because in the societies, in which the final proceeds are shared pro rata by performances, the fewer the rehearsals, the more easily they earn a living.

B G . It comes back, then, to saying that if music must die, it will die of an excess of routine?

AH. You, who habitually frequent concerts, know well enough that the young modern composer's symphony has all the disadvantages as compared to a great classical symphony. The great classical symphony is in the society's library–no difficulties; just go and look up the score, no need even to work, merely re-read certain difficult passages if the conductor is conscientious; and that's it. On the other hand, for the symphony of an unknown, the material has to be rented from the publisher–which is an expense; then, in order to gain some conception of the work–modern scores not being familiar to the orchestra, like those of the repertory–there must be the rehearsal sessions. Now each rehearsal taxes the general budget of the society. There is thus no interest in entering these works on the programme, unless it be to justify the small subsidy. Add to this the fact that the hall will be empty.

BG. One cannot drive the societies to suicide, and it is very difficult to force the public by military means to go to hear contemporary works. Only an orchestra which is both very dependent –because dependent on the State–and independent–because the State will provide substantial subsidies–can sustain contemporary music, in the real sense of the word. The situation of broadcasting orchestras is quite different.

AH. One fine day the symphonic organizations will die. As for chamber music, is it not already virtually dead? How many performances of quartet music does one hear? Naturally, I am not speaking of programmes of Beethoven quartets, followed by the three customary quartets, Ravel, Debussy and Franck, performed by some outside, famous group, on its way through.

BG. Sometimes one of Fauré's.

AH. In the composition contests, students who present a quartet almost always submit an imitation of the quartet of Ravel or Debussy. It could hardly be otherwise, for most of them have never heard any others. How many would know those of

Haydn, Mozart, or Brahms? Even less the most recent ones. But Ravel's quartet they know by heart!

BG. Nevertheless, the performance of Bartók's six quartets by the Vegh quartet filled the auditorium a year and a half ago at the Conservatory.

AH. I am delighted: it is the exception which confirms the rule I proposed above. But there, too, it was the interpreters who were admired more than the works. If the Vegh quartet had been replaced by the X quartet of Paris, should we have seen the same audiences?

BG. I am not sure. Here we return to one of your familiar ideas—the supremacy of the star performer over the text which he or she interprets.

AH. As to piano recitals, that is an even more sensitive topic. In 1949, in recognition of the centenary of Chopin's death, we were presented with a hundred Chopin Festivals. And always the sporting-contest atmosphere, the 'international champions', the 'challengers'.

Examine the statistics on the total of exalted names in the recitals of a single season. It's frightening. I once received a letter from a gentleman in the provinces, a musical amateur. He complained of having heard Chopin's *Sonate funèbre* fifteen times in the same season, and almost as often the *Appassionata*, the *Waldstein* and the *Études Symphoniques*. Another person wrote to me: 'Three pianists appeared in recitals whose programmes showed no great range of imagination: "Works of Chopin" by Jean Doyen; "Works of Chopin" by Marcel Ciampi; "Works of Chopin" by Walter Rummel. Since then, it has only got worse.'

BG. –

AH. Another form of chamber music, the trio, no longer exists. How many can you recall since the retirement of the famous Cortot-Thibaud-Casals trio?

Of course, there are some excuses of a practical nature. The well-known pianist plays alone. His are the total receipts–sometimes lucrative, if it happens to be a famous Chopin recital, attended by all the piano students who are working on the same pieces. But the group has to share, which notably decreases the profits, because expenses also are tripled or quadrupled.

BG. So much pessimism crushes me, I admit. But do you pass on this disillusionment on musical matters to your students in composition?

AH. There I contradict myself. I am convinced of the end of music in the near future, yet I am a professor of composition. I have thirty-seven students at the Normale École de musique. My class always begins– and you can confirm this–with a little speech of which this is roughly the substance:

'Gentlemen, do you sincerely wish to become composers of music? Have you reflected carefully on what awaits you? If you write music, you will not be paid and you will not earn a living. If your father can afford to support you, then nothing prevents you from putting black marks on paper. You will learn that, wherever you go, what you value above all other things will have but a secondary importance for others; they will show no impatience to discover you and your sonata. Your only excuse is to write honestly the music that you wish to express, to bring to it all the pains, all the knowledge, which a man of probity would give to the most serious actions of his life. Suppose for a single moment that you thirty-seven men are–I do not say men of genius, but of talent–and that each one writes in a single year one worthy composition which deserves to be produced; that would unloose a veritable catastrophe in the musical world.'

BG. Most encouraging!

AH. What would you have? Composing is not a profession. It is a mania–a harmless madness, because it is rare to see an unknown composer give way to violent demonstrations and disturbances of the public peace, unless in a concert hall at the performance of a rival's work. More often he is preoccupied, distraught, saddened by the proofs of incomprehension on the part of his contemporaries. If he is not ridiculous because of his arrogance and presumption, he will be as timid as a person afflicted by some abnormality which, it so happens, is not constantly on exhibition for all to see. And there you are!

CHAPTER 3

To Live . . .

*

Everyone has to live? I do not see
the necessity.

BARBEY D'AUREVILLY

BG. To compose music is the finest of professions. Having said
so much, how does one subsist as composer?
AH. Society women, industrialists, bankers, agree that that is a
prosaic problem, unworthy of creative artists: a musician lives
by talent, nay, by genius. Having set this up as an axiom, they
prefer not to look more deeply into the question. They are wise,
because they would be disillusioned, and nothing is so much
dreaded in the ideal realm of the arts as disillusionment!
BG. But since artists rarely live off society ladies—at least, not
always—what do they live on?
AH. Evidently not on music! Seriously, several paths are open to
a composer: a professorship, a civil service position, virtuosity,
or the cinema. He holds a professorship in an institution where he
directs a Conservatory—such was the case with Delvincourt—
or he collects the *grands prix* of Rome, grants to study in the
eternal city—such was Ibert's situation—or still again, like
Henry Barraud, he presides over the destinies of the radio. If
he plays the piano like Rachmaninoff, the violin like Enesco, or

the organ like Marcel Dupré, he is saved. Finally, if he has won a solid notoriety in oratorio, or, preferably, in operetta, it is not impossible that some scenario writer might liven up his next film by giving him credit for concocting two tangos or three waltz tunes.

BG. Is that all?

AH. There is also the hypothetical chance of a certain family fortune. A father who is industrialist, man of business or trade, might very well assist his son to follow a profession which will earn him some successes, perhaps, but certainly not a living.

I shall cite my own example. My father, in Le Havre, was the manager or agent for a large coffee-importing concern. When my studies were completed, he said to me, 'You are entering the firm. You will have very little to do; in the morning you will spend two hours at the Exchange; in the afternoon, you will sign your correspondence; and the rest of the time you can compose music.'

BG. And you did not follow this tempting advice?

AH. I resisted, because I was young, full of enthusiasm, and ridiculously conceited. I said to myself: 'Schubert, Mozart or Wagner would never have accepted such an offer. Sell coffee and compose the *Erlkönig*, the *Magic Flute* or *Parsifal*: they don't belong together!' Note that at that time there was no reason to believe that I might one day command attention by the smallest melody! Nevertheless, I refused the paternal advice. My parents were admirable: in spite of their four children, they accepted the fact that I would embark on a musical career, knowing very well that they must support me for an indefinite number of years, perhaps for my lifetime.

BG. They did not come off so badly.

AH. But contrary to all logic. Almost all the coffee merchants of Le Havre were ruined after the war of 1914. Had I listened to my father, I should have barely made a living as a second violin in Le Havre's Folies-Bergère.

BG. How could anyone, to take another illustration, maintain life as a civil servant and a musician, combining administrative responsibilities with artistic concerns? Either he would sacrifice his creative work to his office, or he would skimp his duty to the state for his vocation. Is not the ideal solution to divide one's artistic life, if possible, into two unequal parts, film music supporting the symphonic?

AH. Divide one's life? Once, before the war, it was possible, even satisfactory, in Germany. There every composer was an orchestral leader, a Kapellmeister, the head of a choral society, or a professor in a school. He earned a very respectable income, which permitted him every year, or nearly every year, to write an oratorio or an opera which was performed in his city, sometimes in the neighbouring city. Charming. In France it was otherwise. All is centred in Paris. If you don't live in Paris, you are unknown. We all recall the sad case of Guy Ropartz who, having been Director of the Conservatory of Nancy, then of Strasbourg, sacrificed a large part of his reputation to his position. He renounced the considerable success he might have had, had he lived in Paris.

As soon as an artist has given sufficient proof of talent, he is assigned one of those honorary posts we mentioned above. Crushed under administrative red-tape and all kinds of drudgery, the unhappy man is swiftly reduced to being incapable of doing any harm—I mean, of writing works which might have found a place on concert programmes or in the lyric theatre, or might have competed with the great German and Italian masters. 'Fonctionnaire! Fonctionnaire!' they might have sung instead of 'Millionaire' in René Clair's film!

BG. All of which adds up to saying that 'serious' music does not feed the man?

AH. Novels, plays, films, often portray the successful composer. He marries the young girl of his love and installs her in a special hotel on the Avenue Bois de Boulogne. I have already vigorously protested against these unforgivable 'inspirations to

composition', the work of ignorant literary hacks. A success at
the Opéra! And behold, you are rich and famous! Idiocy! Was it
once true? Things have changed in half a century. One might
have made a fortune in the lyric theatre when that theatre still
flourished. Massenet lived thus in Paris, Richard Strauss in Germany, and Puccini in Italy. Consider how Massenet earned by
contract 150,000 francs in a year, granted that that is but a
thirtieth of our millions today. The same sum had been set aside
for Verdi, for his *Aida*, composed for the opening of the Italian
Theatre in Cairo. It gives one pause. We know no one today but
butchers or labour contractors who amass such wealth!

Today it is hard to find any who write for the theatre. Opera as
a genre is in its last stages. All that remains are symphonies,
sonatas, and other trifles. If people knew how insignificant are
the royalties that reward the author for his labour! How many
would know that Gabriel Fauré, Director of the Conservatory,
Commander of the Legion of Honour, despite his fame, could
not raise from his author's royalties a sum sufficient to admit him
to a permanent membership in the S.A.C.E.M., the Society of
Authors, Composers, and Editors of Music? That gives one
something to reflect on.

*

A H . Let us take as an example the production of a great work for
chorus, soloists, organ, orchestra, at the Palais de Chaillot–
I mean the work of a man whose reputation is already established.
The expense of hiring a hall, the publicity, the different taxes,
come to a total so high that even if the hall is filled, the operation
will end up with a serious deficit. Do not forget that the State
continues to levy its taxes, thus destroying every chance
of balancing a budget. The same State subsidizes certain associations and groups, such and such performances. Why such
generosity? Because if it allowed the same organizations to go

under, it would lose a sum much greater than the cost of the subsidy. In the end, the State gains on all reckonings.

BG. Your account is so gloomy that I wonder if you are not deliberately exaggerating the black.

AH. To disabuse you I shall produce the figures, and at the outset –if you will forgive me–bring myself into the picture. Imagine that I, as is my unfortunate habit, have composed a symphony or an oratorio with chorus. See me now at work. Why these anxious wrinkles on my brow? What am I seeking? Themes? No. I am saying to myself: 'Will this be produced some day? Hmm! Published? Ha, ha! Replayed? That, never!' Listen. I give you approximately my monologue as I sit before my ruled paper:

'Let me see, I have still enough for . . . yes, three full months. After that, there will be the orchestra to find: five months, working without let-up. There! It is finished. I write the concluding signature. Now my troubles are just beginning! Yes, I'll go and show this to Désormière or to Paray. That means one or two years in their pigeon-holes, that's the inescapable period of waiting; well, works ripen that way, like pears on a fruit tree. Finally, one day the Committee accepts the wonder.

'But the following day, the happy mortal who will direct this masterpiece summons me. He is worried. Is it the Adagio with chorus which bothers him? Will he protest at the 5–4 time? Not at all. He urges me towards his desk and, before my eyes, does some arithmetic. Figures! Always figures!

' "We'll need six rehearsals of the chorus."

' "Fine."

' "Six rehearsals of the chorus–120 choristers at 650 francs per appearance; then a dress rehearsal and a final performance–that's 624,000 francs."[1]

' "Agreed!"

[1] The franc in July, 1950, was valued at 350 francs per dollar. *Translator's note.*

' "Three rehearsals for the orchestra, eighty musicians, plus the dress rehearsal and performance, the conductor's fee, incidental expenses: 775,000 francs; plus 25 per cent for social and treasury taxes."

' "What?"

' "The hall (rehearsals and concert): 165,000. Publicity: 100,000 at least. Fee for the organizer, 50,000. Total 1,654,000 for starting expenses."

' "As much as that?"

' "We can count on taking in from a good hall, at Chaillot, 800,000 francs; but we must subtract taxes, and the entertainment tax (16·25 per cent), copyright (8·8 per cent). From receipts, deduct 200,400. Net receipts will reach 599,000 francs."

' "No more?"

' "Wait a moment, that isn't all; we have to count 300,000 for the social and treasury tax on fees for choristers and instrumentalists. Net receipts will be around 299,000; hence, a deficit of 1,654,000, less 299,000, comes to 1,354,400."

' "Are you really a member of the Beaux-Arts? You will have to ask them yourself to make an effort. Obviously, that will not be easy." '

One million three hundred and fifty-four thousand; one million three hundred thousand, perhaps, by cutting expenses. 1,300,000, a nightmare, which sets the rhythm for the monotonous refrain to my slave labours. 1,300,000, for a single performance; 1,300,000–an obsession, which forces me to lend an ear to the offer of some scenario writer. 1,300,000: let us wind up our oratorio in a hurry, and think about things more serious: a film, two films–one's name on the screen in the space of a lightning flash, some well-mannered music, carefully smothered, which will attract no attention–nothing to fear from the public!

There you have it!

*

BG. Let us suppose that the composer is also a conductor and himself directs.

AH. That will hardly alter the unstable balance of the budget. Shall I cite my own experience again? Once, after a most 'brilliant' concert, it happened to me that, after deducting the various taxes, I found myself the possessor of a sum that would not have allowed me to pay for moving the piano from the firm of Pleyel to the Palais de Chaillot!

BG. Fame is the sunshine of the dead and fortune their consolation!

AH. Such consolation lasts only half a century. Fifty years after the death of a composer his descendants can no longer claim royalties. His works fall into the public domain: after that anyone can earn a living from his work *except the author's relatives*! A banker wills his bank to his son and it remains in the family. But in the domain of the mind the State permits no inheritance. Imagine the immense sums that flow into Austria thanks to Mozart's operas! Or into Germany from the multiplication of Festivals! Again, the only ones excluded from such celebrations are the heirs of the author.

As to the public, this 'domain' which belongs to them is a delusion by which they are mocked at will, as has been sufficiently demonstrated by the eminent jurists, Paul Berthier, Jacques-F. Chartier and Léon Bérard. A single example. When a work which has fallen into the public domain is played at the Opéra or the Théâtre Français, is the price for seats at all reduced? Should we conclude then that only the interpreters are paid and the work worth nothing? Bach and Balzac are in the public domain: try to obtain their complete works; they will cost you more than the works of authors still living. The paper, the ink, the binding, that's what you pay for. The author's thought is worth nothing, materialistically speaking; it is free, over and above the price.

B G. Thus the dead share no better than the living–a disillusioning argument!

A H. The case of the young composer is truly tragic. Suppose one of his works receives a first performance by a concert group. He is required to furnish *without charge* the orchestral parts which represent, not to mention large sums of money, days and nights of labour. Should he become famous, his royalties will not follow the ascending curve of his reputation. It is discouraging. True, the greatest of painters have sold their canvases for a few francs at the outset of their careers; but towards the end of their lives, prices changed, sometimes reaching dizzying heights. Nothing like this for the unhappy musician.

BG. Perhaps he is compensated by the number of concerts?

A H. Performances of modern works are extremely infrequent. I can cite the case of a famous composer, member of the Institute, whose symphony was given a very successful first performance; nevertheless, the second appearance was not until thirty years later. On top of this, the composer, like all independent intellectual workers, was given unusually unfair treatment by the tax-collectors. Not only did he pay the assessments, like everyone else, but all the receipts taken in at the door of the hall, which might have permitted him, if not to earn, at least to reduce the deficit, constituted a first tax taken from him in advance. Until recent years, the rule of a double tax meant that a work performed in England had first to undergo income tax. What was left, transferred to the Society of Authors, which naturally took out its customary commission, was then allotted to the author: an expense to him, that is, to pay tax on the learned professions, then tax on the revenue. In certain cases, there remains for him hardly one per cent of the royalty originally set aside. Furthermore, these amounts reach him after a delay of several years. With more recent laws, aimed at forbidding exchange between countries, the more surely to ruin Europe, the delays are only so much the greater.[1] What is more, a number of governments cold-bloodedly refuse to release the smallest royalties to the authors. There does exist, however, an International Confederation of Societies of Authors and Composers which battles energetically for an equitable distribution in all countries of the world. If authors and composers could obtain the rightful remuneration for their work, they would present a less doleful figure. But how battle against a legally organized exploitation?

BG. *O infortunatos nimium ...*[2]

AH. Even Latin poetry can do very little to sweeten my bitterness!

---

[1] 'Meanwhile, these bureaucratic extremes have taken a truly grotesque form: for example, the material for a performance transported from Switzerland to France must pay the customs duties going and coming; musical scores passing from Switzerland into Germany for simple corrections are equally subject to duty. Add to these shabby tricks the tendency of several governments to find pretexts for customs duties, plus the lack of machinery for establishing any direction in the realm of the arts and sciences.

'Artists who live in Switzerland suffer still, as they did formerly, from the system of a tax at the source, following in this the example of England, certain states of the Commonwealth, the U.S.A. and Austria. The consequence is an insupportable double tax. The net receipts from the author's royalties, or those deriving from concerts of Swiss interpreters in England, are submitted first to a tax at source of around 45 per cent; the remaining 55 per cent is again submitted to Swiss assessment, so that an artist is fortunate if anything remains at the end to reward him for his effort.' Extract from the *Bulletin de l'Association des Musiciens Suisses*. Report of the Committee on Practice, 1950. *Author's note.*

[2] 'O too unfortunate'—paraphrase of Virgil. *Translator's note.*

CHAPTER 4

The Drama and Mystery
of Publication

*

To compose a masterpiece is nothing;
to get it published is everything!

STENDHAL

BG. What an abyss between literary and musical publication!
To get a book published is relatively easy; to get a score in print
is a dramatic experience. Why this difference?
AH. There is always the question of supply and demand. And
fewer and fewer musical scores are purchased. There are actually
several causes for this. For one thing, it has become very difficult
to read modern music; and this increasing difficulty has discouraged the amateur whose favourite pastime was once sight-
reading at the piano. Fifty years ago, in every middle-class home
where there was a piano we should have found *Carmen*, *Faust*,
Manon and *Werther*. But since *Pelléas*, why buy illegible scrawls?
Why go to such trouble when the radio is at hand, docile, inexhaustible, richer than any library? Let's not compete with the
virtuoso whom we shall hear this evening on the waves! How can
an amateur undertake the study of a Schoenberg quartet, when
the reading and the performance are equally arduous?–so arduous
that the sale of such scores is practically non-existent!

BG. Even if the composer is famous?

AH. Do not doubt it. Granted there are on the face of the globe four or five composers of whom, because of the rapid rise of their reputation and a widespread respect, a publisher might say to himself: 'I cannot do other than publish his quartet or his quintet.'

BG. Is the publisher a patron or a business man?

AH. He can and must be both. The mechanics of financing a musical publication is very delicate. I take one illustration: the publisher Sénart who published every three months a collection entitled *Chamber Music*, containing a sonata for piano and violin, a sonata for piano and violoncello, a trio or quartet with piano, and some little piano pieces. Subscription for this publication was the same as that for a magazine, at a very modest cost.

BG. Did it prosper?

AH. Are you joking? The search for composers was almost as burdensome as the pursuit of subscriptions. What a task, to find every year four violin sonatas, four sonatas for violoncello, four trios or quartets, let us not say excellent, but worthy of publication! Soon running out of manuscripts, Sénart fell to publishing texts of doubtful interest. Even a mediocre composer who appeared with a sonata rolled under his arm looked like a saviour!

BG. As for subscribers—

AH. They said to themselves: 'I'd rather spend a little more for sonatas which I enjoy.'

BG. What are the 'best-sellers' for the great publishing houses: Durand, Leduc, Lemoine, Salabert and others?

AH. First, instruction books, treatises, solfèges (singing exercises)—it's amazing how many of these are sold—collections of piano and violin exercises, then classical works revised and annotated by top names of the musical world. Chopin revised by Cortot heads the list of sellers in this field.

As a sideline to his very important stock-in-trade of symphonic works Salabert has always been the greatest publishing house for light music—songs and operettas. A song success enables him to publish a symphony. In this way 'light' music helps the 'great' to survive. But if commercial music is more remunerative than the other in the short run, it is also usually the first to disappear. Almost every year its repertory is renewed, and it is naturally much less burdensome to handle than operas and concertos.

All this permits the publisher to consider the publication of the works of great composers of genius who still amuse themselves by writing sonatas and symphonies.

B G . Let us take an illustration: you compose a symphony for full orchestra; it is wonderfully received, praised by the press, directed by a great conductor, esteemed by your colleagues—is that not the height of approbation? You take your symphony to a publisher. What happens?

A H . Let us accept your exaggerated hypotheses—though I beg of you, do not always take me as an illustration. I happen to be fortunate in having some publishers who are also friends, and who manage to convince me that the publication of one of my manuscripts is the height of their wishes. That costs them dearly, nevertheless, by very reason of the rarity of a specialized crafts-manship.

The initial investment will not be covered until long years have passed, and then only on condition that the composer is known and played abroad. If all goes well, the publisher's children will see the dawning of profits—at least, if the composer does not die too soon, for after all, fifty years, then public domain! I mention foreign outlets, for the investment will return to the fold from foreign markets. In the great man's native country, it is deemed quite natural to solicit his material without charge. The foreign approach in such matters is more normal. In America especially, outlets are numerous, in view of the many concert groups and university orchestras. I add, too, that the exchange is favourable.

Under such circumstances, the publication of music becomes less visionary; it becomes a reality set on a business foundation.

There is still another obstacle to the sale of music, quite a practical one: that is the inconvenient format of these thin, fragile sheets, which generally manage to arrive torn. Those who own a library know how difficult it is to shelve them. Finally, these few leaves cost an exorbitant price because of the limited printings. Further, international exchanges are all but paralysed by the obstacles raised by customs offices and Bureaus of Exchange, whose function is to ruin the world. Hence, royalties paid out for producing a work reach either publisher or author only after a considerable delay. This matter I have already treated in a previous chapter.

B G. Fortunately, there are recordings—

A H. Yes, recordings have the advantage of a tremendous distribution. But they are subjected to the same rulings on international exchange. It is almost impossible to export French recordings into America, for customs duties are too high.

B G. The study score—

A H. The pocket score is indeed a useful device. It sells well. Young people, especially abroad, build libraries of little scores as well as record libraries, which enable them to know these works well.

B G. Let us return to publication, properly speaking, and examine the situation of a composer without a name who has just composed a work recognized as excellent. What happens to it?

A H. First of all, he must have it performed. The difficulties in the way of a first hearing—usually without a follow-up—are less than they once were. Once there were but three orchestras in Paris. Their repertory was desperately classical. A composer of the older generation told me of submitting a work to Colonne with a view to a first hearing. Colonne looked at it, refused it, and returned it with these words: 'What troubles me is that if I do not play you, no one will.' Today the radio offers an important outlet: more and more it aids composers by sometimes furnishing the material orchestra at its own expense; in some cases, it even pays for the work.

BG. A miracle!

AH. As for publication, that's another matter. Engraving is scarcely done any more. But duplication and photostatic copies are in themselves very expensive. Further, nine times out of ten the work, even if excellent, remains in private hands. If some foreign orchestra asks permission to perform it, what then does the composer do? Must he copy it himself or pay for setting up the material? In the first case, he wastes time, in the second, money. For a professional man, a matter of X hours of labour is needed to transcribe the text for a symphony with full orchestra. Shall he lose X hours or spend Y francs? The alternatives are not encouraging. To part with his manuscript is to abandon his child; obviously, that is out of the question!

*

BG. How is a contract drawn up between composer and publisher?

AH. The most equitable system, that in use elsewhere for literary publication, is almost everywhere adopted: namely, royalties paid on copies sold. Such royalty never exceeds a 10 per cent rate, from which two per cent is deducted for damaged copies. The royalty is therefore in actuality reduced to eight per cent. For an extremely well-known composer, the publisher customarily grants an advance or an account on future royalties.

BG. For the reader who is more familiar with literature than music, let us compare a musician with a man of letters—for example, Olivier Messiaen with Hervé Bazin—though the *Banquet Céleste* (the 'Heavenly Banquet') is far more edifying than the *Vipère au Poing* (the 'Viper in Hand')! The *Vipère au Poing* saw a printing of 150,000 copies, while Messiaen's *Préludes*, composed in 1928, on a printing of 500 copies, did not begin to sell, and then very meagrely, until 1946, after the success of his *Petites Liturgies*. It took eighteen years for Messiaen, a reputable and even famous composer, to sell a few copies of his delightful *Préludes*.

AH. I can cite you also the case of a totally unknown young painter who gained over 100,000 francs at his first showing, at a time when the franc was valued above its stated rate. Consider, by comparison, that Messiaen had a world-wide reputation, that he had been invited to America, and that he had experienced important command performances. His name is famous, he is a professor at the Conservatory, and yet–And you say that I exaggerate when I pity the lot of the musician? In support of my thesis, and by way of proof, here is a little table released by the firm of Durand. It shows the number of copies issued and the curve of sales for certain titles of contemporary music:

Composer	Work	Edition	Figure and Date of 1st Printing	Date Exhausted
Debussy	*First Arabesque*	Piano	400–1891	1903
Debussy	*Children's Corner*	Piano	1,000–1908	1909
Ravel	*Histoires Naturelles*	Piano and Voice	500–1907	1913
Ravel	*Mother Goose*	Piano, 4 hands	500–1910	1912
Ravel	*Bolero*	Piano (short score)	2,000–1929	1929
Messiaen	*Eight Preludes*	Piano	500–1910	Not exhausted
Milhaud	*2nd Symphonic Suite*	Orchestral Score	100–1921	Not exhausted

Thus it took a dozen years to dispose of 400 copies of Debussy's *First Arabesque*, which every pianist plays! That 2,000 copies of a popular masterpiece like Ravel's *Bolero* (in its piano version; that is, in the most accessible, if not the most flattering version) should sell out in one year is an event without precedent in the annals of music publication. But think of Proust and Maurois: how many literary men are favoured over musicians!

BG. If I understand correctly, a young composer faces the

following dilemma: 'Get yourself published and you will be known–Get yourself known and you will be published.'

AH. The old formula has always the force of law.

There is no common ratio between the reputation of certain musicians and their financial resources. I know some who have scarcely sold a copy: on the other hand, the halo of misunderstood innovators is bestowed on them by foreign musical reviews (there are no longer such reviews in France).

BG. The warmth with which people discuss a recently published book is not necessarily dependent on the number printed. If 500 people buy a book, if thirty others acquire a score, that suffices to feed discussion, even argument. Think of the free-lance journalists, all those who discourse without having read a line of the novel or the score.

AH. Let us stick to the practical issues. There is no doubt that the publisher Gallimard made much more money out of the detective stories called the *Série Noire*, than he did from the works of the members of the French academy in his *Editions de la Nouvelle Revue Française*.

BG. The same in music, a great symphony 'returns' less to Mme Salabert as publisher than a frightful money-maker like–

AH. No names, please! Besides, to be entirely just, let us say that the profit seeker is only temporarily 'interesting'. The future is with the serious composer–no–do not laugh!

BG. Considering the obstacles put in the way of music publication, one wonders if there are not men of talent who have never had a chance to be discovered.

AH. I do not think so. There are so many prizes, competitions, trial auditions, that the unknown talent, since he is hunted out on all sides, must some day be discovered, in spite of himself. Often no prize is awarded in these competitions, because the level of work submitted is too inferior. Musicians with a certain standing do not like to risk their reputations thus.

BG. The unfortunate thing is that outstanding talent is so rarely found with an income.

AH. The truly sad thing is this: there are in France several hundred writers, of diverse reputations, who live by publishing their works–which is normal. Almost anyone can read a book, but rare are those who can read music. There are not ten composers whose lot is comparable to that of their literary colleagues.

BG. Not ten? In France, or in the whole world?

AH. Say not a dozen on the face of the globe. That is not a brilliant showing. You see from what authentic springs my troubled spirit is nourished. Here, as before, we must choose between optimism and clear-sightedness.

CHAPTER 5

Matters of Profession[1]

*

A publisher asked me to prepare a book
on the technique of painting. I wrote it.
When I re-read it, I learned how to paint.

SALVADOR DALI

In a study entitled *My Profession* one must have the courage
to treat of all that pertains to the profession, including somewhat
technical matters such as are of great importance to specialists.
Those who are not interested will skip this chapter: a book is
not a symphony which must be endured in its entirety. In the
words of the delightful Duvernois: the descriptions in a novel are
there solely to give the reader practice in the art of skipping.

I shall treat here of the anomalies, the incoherences, the
antiquated practices of musical notation, all very dear to the old
autocrats who teach music. They are so proud to know something,
these old professors whose job it is in all corners of the globe to
disgust students with music, and who are the more proud of
their art as it is the more inconvenient and difficult to apply.

Personally, I have already been involved in a squabble over the
subject of Nicolas Obouhov's notation, which I persist in thinking
very timely. This stand has caused me to be rebuked.

[1] Here as elsewhere below, I have turned to the monologue. I apologize.
Author's note.

The simplest music is already difficult to read. Why then complicate it further by absurd conventions? 'To drive off the stupid,' replies Satie, who amuses himself by writing in the treble clef what should be in the bass clef, and vice versa, in his *Uspud*, 'Christian ballet for one person'. The 'stupid' being in the great majority, *Uspud* has quite deservedly remained unknown.

Obouhov was chiefly reproached for basing his system on keyboard instruments–piano, organ, celesta and harpsichord–and for using the same notation to indicate F sharp and G flat, for example. Strong emotions, great indignation in the ranks of high competence! What would become of the famous 'interval' which still differentiates G flat from F sharp? It appeared that its disappearance would provoke the disappearance of the whole 'ethos'. I have never received an answer to my request for particulars, for the simple reason that in every orchestral score every bar will show a flattened note doubling for a sharp. Thus the identical melody played by a clarinet in B flat may be written to sound in G flat, while the violin which doubles it may play in F sharp. As an illustration, in the final chord of *Tristan*, the horns in F play B flats and D flats, while the rest of the orchestra plays in B major. No one is scandalized by this inconsistency in musical orthography. Everyone deliberately ignores the fact that the written sign is nothing but a convention to make the performance of musical works possible. Literary artists, less narrowly inhibited, make use of shorthand and stenotype. Does that alter the thought of whatever they may be trying to express? But the high priests of Euterpe insist that we must force ourselves to use four different signatures to indicate the same sound: the sharp, the flat, the double sharp, the double flat. How simple and logical!

I shall not dwell further on this matter, but shall only mention in passing that until Beethoven's time whenever the cello moved into the higher registers and made use of the G clef without first utilizing the C clef, the part was written an octave higher than the sound desired. Why? Mystery and tradition, happily less in evidence today.

I might add the same comment on the notation for choruses, in the four clefs–three of C and one of F–which d'Indy was still employing. But this complication was reserved for orchestral scores, no doubt for the edification of conductors. For the piano reduction, all is re-transcribed into the G clef.

Simplification, logic, economy!

*

Another anomaly uselessly complicating reading is what I shall call 'black writing', examples of which may be found in the greatest masters, Bach, Beethoven, etc. Would not the variations in the Sonata, Op. 111, *Adagio semplice*, have gained from a less forbidding notation than the following?

Ex.1

But, as Lady Macbeth says, 'What's done is done.' I try only to convince future Beethovens.

In classical music, which modulates relatively little, it was the custom to indicate accidentals–sharps or flats–appropriate to the principal key at the beginning of the staves. However, during a period still quite recent, in which modulation is continual, the great masters have remained faithful to this antiquated habit. Thus, in *Ariane et Barbe-Bleue* by Paul Dukas (who was certainly not given to joking), we find at the beginning of the second act a signature of six flats whose existence is immediately ignored, and yet they remain clinging there like so many abandoned sausages, with the notes embellished by sharps or naturals as needed. The result is a printing of around ninety-eight accidentals per page, useless and confusing:

Ex. 2

Furthermore, a few pages farther on, these flats give way to a signature of sharps, and immediately these notes are embellished with untimely flats:

Ex. 3

Another observation of a pedant. In the era of *bel canto*, it was the custom to prolong each syllable over two or more notes. But today we are generally satisfied with one note per syllable. Nevertheless, we have piously retained the custom of indicating the vocal part in separated quavers or semiquavers, without linking them in groups, with bars or 'flags', as is the usage in instrumental music; all of which makes reading more difficult, and gives rise to constant confusion for singers whose talent for sight-reading is often limited. No one can deny that of the following notations, the first (*a*) is more readable than the second (*b*):

El-les sont là !   nour-ri-ce, nour-rice où es-tu?

(*Ariane et Barbe-Bleue*)
page 92

One may find a hundred illustrations even more typical in modern scores.

Such endlessly increasing obstacles in the reading of contemporary music should incite composers to seek the most rational means of notation. Some have understood this; others have exhibited a kind of childish coyness in exaggerating the difficulties. They are in error, not only for their own works, which discourage both amateurs and professionals, but for the cause of music as a whole. Thus Olivier Messiaen, whose scores scarcely err by excess of simplicity, has invented a new complication in writing, for which he has never been able to give me an explanation. When he wishes to tie two chords, he does not indicate the tie immediately after the first chord, as would be logical, but only before the second. Should there happen to be a page to turn between these two chords, one would have to be unusually endowed with prescience to guess that the second chord is tied to the first, and is not to be struck a second time.

I come now to the problem of what is called transposing instruments, a term which is no longer normal in our day, because all these instruments are chromatic, and because it is literally absurd to assign them one key in preference to another. We know how this came about. Before the invention of pistons and changeable crooks for horns, a horn or a trumpet could sound naturally only the harmonic series determined by the length of its tubing. These instruments were then in E flat or E natural. The bell could be stopped by the use of the fist, and the sounds thus produced would round out the scale of the key, for better or for worse. In order to compensate for the inconvenience of these muffled sounds, which differed from natural sounds, composers adopted the custom of composing for each instrument in a different fundamental key. The score, as Gevaert had already pointed out in 1885, thus became a laborious task to read. But today, since all instruments alike are capable of playing chromatic sounds, why conserve the old system? All horn players now play on the same length of tubing, that of the horn in F. Why in F? Because of the fundamental, which is no longer of the least importance, since it is followed by the whole chromatic scale. Why not then write the horn parts realistically, in C, as parts are written for the flute or trombone? Yet, quite the contrary, a further idiotic complication has been added. If the score is written in the treble clef, one must read the text a fifth lower, and as soon as it moves into the bass clef, a fourth higher. Widor pointed out this ridiculous convention more than thirty years ago in his *Treatise on Orchestration*: 'Imagine (he wrote) two horns in unison. If the first plays in the treble clef and the second in the bass clef, what is unison to the ear will be written as an octave for the eye. O triumph of illogic! Why not make the bass clef continue naturally into the treble clef?' But that would assuredly be too obvious!

In his *Nocturnes* and *La Mer*, Debussy still wrote the trumpets in F. I asked the first trumpet of the Opéra on what instrument he played these works. 'We play everything on the trumpet in C,' he replied. 'But from the parts written in F?' 'Yes. What would you have us do? We transpose!' Durand and Company continue imperturbably to print parts for the instrument in F, which no longer exists!

Simplification, logic, economy!

*

The same problems arise and the same idiocies reappear when we turn to the clarinets, the saxophones, and the English horns. The origin of this confusion is military. Soldiers belonging to musical groups and military bands already had enough difficulty in reading the treble clef. Yet, at that time, as initiated by the genial Sax, all was written in that clef. In an orchestral score, this brings about humorous results. You might see a bass-saxophone or a contra-bass tuba part written like a concerto part for violin, with added lines above the stave. Again, this might have had its excuse a hundred years ago, but not today!

You will find among the virtuosos of the baton some conductors who will assure you: 'A score written entirely in the key of C is to me unreadable, so accustomed am I to reading transposed parts.' You have only to reply to them, calmly: 'Well, then, a whole series of classical works are closed to you, for Mozart, Beethoven, Mendelssohn, Schumann, Liszt, and others very often wrote for the clarinets and horns in C. But you cannot read these parts—or perhaps it escaped your notice, when you were studying them, that they, too, were in C?'

If you wish to amuse yourself, put on your stand certain scores from the period of Meyerbeer, where you will find the four horns playing, for example, the first in B natural (high), the second in F, the third in E, the fourth in B flat (low). Ask the conservators of a healthy tradition to reduce these to a piano score. I promise you some amusing surprises!

Let us try, then, to be as clear as possible. Schoenberg and Prokofiev were among the first to abandon these outmoded concepts. The score is a sound-image, and not a picture puzzle. The written sound must be the one that will be heard by the ear, whatever the arbitrary notation used for the given instruments. Let us overhaul the usages which no longer have a reason for existing today.

I still recall the complaints expressed by some older musicians in the orchestra: 'Monsieur, here there is a G sharp, where before there is a G flat. So we shall have to put a natural before the sharp, to show that the flat is cancelled.' Innovations require a long time for their adoption in a realm where routine is mistress.

Finally, I should like to call the attention of budding composers to a custom which is already terribly dated: that of a perpetual and excessive changing of time. A number of great masters have made use of this and abused it. They confuse rhythm with prosody. Time should play the role of the highway mile-post. To lengthen or curtail these, according to the changes in land-scape, would be nonsense. Why deliberately complicate the performance? The very composers who condemn orchestral conductors for being bewildered by this labyrinth of useless complication, when they come to direct their own scores, tran-scribe entire pages into the same time, to avoid catastrophe! The most complex rhythms can be indicated within the frame of two, three, or four beats per measure. The performance could only be improved, without forcing these burdensome calculations upon the interpreters, for they destroy all feeling of freedom. Furthermore, the kind of writing in which 7/32 time is blended into 5/1 time does not dazzle anyone. Therefore it is unnecessarily pretentious.

Simplification, logic, economy!

*

May I be permitted to formulate once again a few wishes for the future? For one thing, I gladly welcome the introduction of saxophones and alto horns into the symphony orchestra. The orchestra has too long retained the classic or romantic organization. The high clarinet (in E flat) and the small trumpet (in D) are still rare instruments except in a very large orchestra. On the other hand (and I beg the pardon of the players), I should without regrets witness the disappearance of an instrument as unpleasing as the double bassoon. Its contribution to the bass is not sufficient; it is weak and ungainly in the soft passages. The device known as *ondes Martenot*[1] could replace it with advantage. This instrument has a power, a speed of utterance, which is not to be compared with those gloomy stove-pipes looming up in orchestras, logically but mistakenly called *haut-bois* (high wood) by all laymen because of their dimensions.[2] Furthermore, the Martenot apparatus can reproduce most of the tone quality of the present instruments, and that on a practically limitless scale. It could thus replace, in most instances, a number of desks of now doubtful contribution. Let us react with courage against idiotic routine and a false respect for tradition in its dying stages.

[1] Webster: *ondes musicales* or *ondes Martenot*: 'a melodic electrophone capable of producing quarter and eighth notes [crotchets and quavers]'. *Petit Larousse*: 'A melodic instrument whose sound is produced electrically, and which can change tone quality at the will of the operator.' The instrument is named after its inventor. *Translator's note.*

[2] The *hautbois* (unhyphenated) refers to the oboe and not to the bassoon. The oboe is a *high*-pitched *wood*wind instrument, whereas the layman assumes *haut-bois* to mean woodwind that looms high. *Translator's note.*

CHAPTER 6

Intermission:
Music and the Ladies

*

'What a masterpiece *Pelléas* is: I am
madly in love with it,' cried Madame
de Cambremer!

MARCEL PROUST

After a series of mostly disgruntled considerations, it seems
only fair to point out that there are some good moments in a
composer's life. As a matter of fact, some delightful people
inhabit that world.

In the first rank, I should be happy to place those ladies whose
passionate concern is the fine arts, especially music.

I am not proposing the foolish project of writing the appropriate book: *Great Ladies and Music*. That would require an
erudition I completely lack, and a memory sustained by a
historical knowledge beyond my obviously deplorable limitations.
Such little as I might be able to summon would be soon reduced to
a very few items: Marie Antoinette's patronage of Gluck,
Madame d'Epinay's opinion that the young Mozart was not
without talent, the Princess of Metternich's forcing the Opéra
to produce *Tannhäuser*, Madame Verdurin's efforts for the
performance of Vinteuil's *Sonata* in the salons. Even so much
will suffice to indicate the very laudable activities of the fair sex.

Nor need I dwell on those fervent cults of admirers who surround the celebrated orchestral leader, the virtuoso pianist, or, when he still existed, the powerful tenor whose throat provoked such noble swoonings. There, too, the ladies are only too much in evidence.

Those whom I would crown with glory are the friends of the select, who loyally attend the first performance, the private concert, which could have no existence without their faithful presence.

Ah! if we had to count on men alone, crushed by their daily burdens and their material cares, our concert halls would soon be deserted or transformed into uncomfortable sleeping quarters!

But the women understand that they have a mission to fulfil. They buy tickets, and bring others with them, sparing neither time nor labour. More admirable still, during the most favourable twilight hours, they refuse to surrender themselves to certain pleasurable activities– if their years still permit such games– suggested to them by those young men, unfortunately becoming ever more rare, who do not have a resolved aversion to the sex to which they owe their existence. And for what? To be present in some little auditorium, overheated in summer and glacial in winter, at a generally catastrophic performance of frightful combinations of sounds, of which they still have the courage to say: 'How interesting!'

*

These priceless listeners fall into two categories. First, there are those who organize a group and take control. These are found in every city of any size, directing opinion with authority. They preside over Committees for tenth-of-a-whole-tone music, the Societies for the glorification of some forgotten precursor. They offer whisky to music critics for the encouragement of an attentive ear. They lavish their most irresistible smiles on rich industrialists and friends of their husbands, to gather the necessary funds to organize a gala affair for the 'Antithematic Fifteen'. Their persuasive charms lure in the old, enfeebled academician and the world's heavyweight champion. After two hours of boredom, courteously concealed by the guests, they extract from them their enthusiasm for abstract art.

The second category shines by discretion. Ardent candidates wait in the shadows, though impatiently, to take their place among the elect whose word or smile can launch a career or crush a reputation. These ladies will be the vigilant friends of 'the young' (everyone knows that in the realm of music one remains 'young' for a long time). By tactful praises they will impart the impression that he is already 'somebody', that he is the victim of a neglect which renders him equal to the greatest. They will untiringly introduce him to all who might be useful to him: from an orchestral player to a member of the Institute. They will carry self-denial to the point of boosting his merits to the very rich old lady who has the reputation of covering the deficit of the meetings. In short, they will nourish him spiritually and materially, with a disinterestedness which cannot be sufficiently praised.

To say that all these ladies combine competence with good will would be perhaps an exaggeration. We do not ask that much of them. Their convictions are, on the whole, sincere, at least at the moment of their expression.

*

In recognition of their inexhaustible kindnesses, I should like to recount a few personal anecdotes. I hope that no one would want to detect in them an irony quite foreign to me, and, indeed, quite out of place.

When still a young beginner, I was summoned to one of those salons where so many reputations are created, and graciously invited by the mistress of the house to present a sonata for piano and violin of my own authorship. Some surprise was evinced when I announced that I should play the violin part and one of my friends would accompany me on the piano. Our little performance was given a flattering reception, and the hostess asked in the most innocent way possible: 'But who composed the piano part?'

I admitted modestly that it was also my own work. The enthusiasm of my questioner mounted by several degrees: 'Imagine, Adhémar, he composed the piano part also, and yet he cannot play it. It is simply stupendous!'

'But, my dear,' her husband replied, 'that is customary.' Nevertheless, the incredulity persisted, causing me, no doubt, to be classed among the tiresome musicians, but as one whose skill could not be questioned.

Another time, a dancer (from the Opéra, if you please) contributed her part to a matinée organized by the Salon d'Automne. She danced a little ballet which André Hellé and I had composed. But, quite understandably, a star cannot sacrifice her personal career to modern music. So the performance concluded with three Chopin *Mazurkas*. As the audience was leaving, a lady whom I knew very slightly came to me and, clasping my hands, exclaimed with feeling: 'Your little ballet was simply ravishing! Yes! Yes! I assure you! I was not so crazy about the opening, but the three pieces at the end—'

'I am greatly pleased, Madam; and what proof of the infallibility of your taste. They were three *Mazurkas* by Chopin.'

I received in reply a sympathetic smile: 'Ah! that is just like you. You say that out of modesty!'

Some years later, I was arriving one evening to dine with a titled lady, who immediately cried out: 'You dear man! I heard the other day your *Nabucodonosor* on the radio. Heavens! what splendour, it's a sublime masterpiece, it's—'

Recognizing that we were slipping into a dangerous miscomprehension, I made an effort to rectify matters, and, catching my breath, I exclaimed in turn: 'You mean that you heard the *Nabucodonosor* by Tarticol and Frisenouille, or by Frisenouille and Tarticol.'

There was a brief silence, and I heard a very calm voice: 'Oh! it was by Frisenouille and Tarticol. Heavens! What a bore! What terrible cacophony!'

Such are the things that must be said in high society. The lady knew artists and, even better, musicians. She knew that nothing soothes their spirits like a slashing attack on a colleague, and that such is the sweetest of music to their ears. Oh, no matter what we do, these fine ladies will be there to revive us, even though the Tour de Nesle no longer exists.[1]

[1] Apparently a reference to the legend that linked the Tour de Nesle with the princesses who had their lovers for the night tossed from the ramparts. *Translator's note.*

CHAPTER 7

Spirit and Matter

*

The words I use are those of every day
and yet they are no longer the same.
These flowers are your flowers, and you
say that you do not recognize them. And
these feet are your feet, but look! I walk
on the sea and I tread the waters of the
sea in triumph!

PAUL CLAUDEL

B G . Now we shall speak of the condition or state of the composer. That is a word which permits of two quite different
interpretations. There is the material state, the means by which
a modern composer can live and, on occasion, prosper. This
aspect we have already treated at some length. There is also the
mental state, which, without giving rise to deep concern,
poses some problems.

A H . The fact is that, for the average man, the act of composing
music remains an incomprehensible thing. 'Well then, is it not
true that when you compose, you try to find on your piano
something that will make a piece; but when it's a piece for an
orchestra, you can't play all the instrumental parts at the same
time?'

I try to explain that composing sound has to be done first in
the mind, and then be consigned to paper in its larger outlines.
'But without hearing the notes played?' All the more so because
I do not, so to speak, play the piano. 'You are obliged then to

have someone else play it?' No, because that is a mental operation that takes place in the brain of the composer. I do not mean to say that the checking of certain passages on the piano is not useful, if only to help the logical sequence of the different elements, to be used somewhat as a guide.

When you read a book, you are not obliged to pronounce the words aloud. They are heard in your mind. It is the mind, the thought-process, which must create music, and not the fingers wandering at random over the keys. Nevertheless, research on the piano can be fruitful, especially for composers who are skilful instrumentalists and given to improvisation. Schumann condemned this technique, but probably a Chopin or a Liszt made use of the practice. It can have excellent results. In such a case, chance becomes an inspiration, for the first rough draft is re-used, recast, improved, made more exact, by the musical knowledge of the composer. I can well imagine the following example: a composer seated before his keyboard striking chords. Suddenly, he may be charmed by a sequence of two or more of these chords. They will then serve him as a base for the whole harmonic character of a composition. Berlioz conceived a melodic line and then worked out the harmonization on his guitar. This explains the tendency to homophony so characteristic of him. Bach and the polyphonists could very rarely have made use of this procedure.

To the uninitiated the reading of a musical text without an instrument appears to be a marvellous accomplishment. A friend told me with astonishment how, on a train, he had seen a singer learning her role despite the lack of a piano. Remember further that to read an orchestral score is infinitely less easy than to read a literary text, and that it takes long training to acquire this skill. To be convinced you have only to observe how certain conductors of orchestras read their scores. The marks on a score are numerous, and the eye is forced to range over a very considerable space, since some thirty staves have to be read simultaneously from top to bottom of a page. Actually, it is natural enough that others should be astonished at what is rightly the speciality of our profession, and that they should say to us: 'What, you look at the notes, and you hear what they mean?'

All this is less apparent in popular music. There we very frequently find composers who have no technical knowledge. They play 'airs' on the piano which have come to them, and which often will soon be 'on every lip'. These are usually rather short pieces, almost always of the same form—verse, refrain. Such writers are dependent on collaborators who edit their improvisations, harmonize them, orchestrate them. On the one hand is the inventor of ideas; on the other, the technician who builds the piece from these ideas.

In American film music this practice has taken on the status of a tradition. It is perfectly legitimate, because the men who have a knack for melody are not necessarily practitioners. When music draws closer to business methods, then all talents take on a different colouring. We have never required Ford or Citroën to mount their coaches personally on the chassis because they personally conceived and perfected the motor; nevertheless, they put their names on the car.

Let us return to symphonic music. The masses have always been amazed at the existence of the deaf composer. It is not impossible that a great part of the admiration accorded Beethoven derives from his infirmity. In truth, aside from the tragic aspects of such a situation, a creator's inability ever to hear a *performance* of his own work must raise some real technical problems for him. Beethoven progressively forgot the purely aural aspects of certain dispositions. We may discover this in the writing for voices in the *Missa Solennis* or in the *Ninth Symphony*. We may observe it equally in the wide gap between right and left hand in his style of writing for the piano, and especially in the paradoxical harmonization of the *anacrusis* or notes preceding the first downbeat.

Nevertheless, this had no real influence on the essential quality of his thought. I should be tempted to assert that this very deafness, which walled him off within himself, aided the concentration of his genius and detached him from the insipidities and banalities of his times.

By chance, I ran across an old number of the magazine, *Die Musik*, devoted to Beethoven, and containing an article by Dr J. Niemack on the deafness of the master. He cites a specific example: the central passage of the *Cavatina* of the String Quartet, Op. 130, in which the first violin, in a strangely broken rhythm, gives voice to a melodic line marked by Beethoven as *Beklemmt* ('anguished'). 'Ask a cardiologist to listen to this passage,' says Dr Niemack, 'and ask him if he recognizes this rhythm.'

'Naturally,' he will answer. 'It is the heart-beat of an arteriosclerotic, whose heart is affected by a compensatory insufficiency.'

Deafness rendered Beethoven the more sensitive to the sound of his own heartbeats. Dr Niemack wonders, as a sequel, if the aesthetician would consider as at all useful such reproductions of the phenomena of illness.

*

B G. It is true that the creative process remains identical, whether it is a matter of music or painting or poetry. But the writer employs the language of every day. The sculptor and the painter, though by distortion, reproduce a tangible reality. But a musician, on the contrary, creates out of nothing; therefore composition gives the layman the illusion of a miracle.

A H. When a profession meets with ignorance, it is either thought to be very easy or it is esteemed extraordinary. I myself have on my conscience some conversations with painters which enraged them. I said to them: 'How easy your art is! You reproduce a model which you have observed. For a whole lifetime, you can paint three apples on a plate with the excuse that Cézanne painted three apples on a plate. You can place these three apples before you and reproduce them. You have a concrete model. You may paint a still life, representing a bottle of wine, a pipe, a bit of sausage; or you sketch a wholly nude or a beautifully clothed woman. All is within reach of your sight.' The genius of the sculptor consists of giving to a body which he knows anatomically a life and spirit which will express its personality. He, too, has the model before his eyes while he works. The musician must first invent his model and reproduce it afterwards. If I desire to compose a sonata for piano and violin, I have absolutely nothing before my eyes or in my memory. I must invent everything.

BG. Do not other sonatas for piano and violin furnish you with models?

AH. One cannot be satisfied with reproducing the form. Another sonata may, indeed, serve as a model, but the important thing is the actual sound, the themes, the melodies, the rhythms. If I copy, I am a conscious imitator, but in vain.

BG. Our ancestors were not so punctilious.

AH. True. Men of talent, like Bach, transcribed the works of their predecessors and were inspired by them. Today a personal contribution is expected of the composer; it is quite fruitless to imitate the sonata of another. One must invent a personal model in the abstract, and construct it ideally. But this model will have no definite form before it is realized, for according to the material employed, the model will shift its form. The statue all of a sudden will have another nose. Its aspect, its proportions, will shift, and will oblige me to transform the beautiful nude into a leopard.

BG. So, after having derided the childish conceptions the public holds about the composer, we come around to supplying arguments for the victims of our irony! For in the process which you describe, there is an astonishing succession of operations. It is a kind of wizardry!

AH. Fortunately, there is in music a large part of wizardry, of the inexplicable. It is not comparable to any other art. Our ancestors showed wisdom when they excluded music from the fine arts. On one side, music. On the other, painting, sculpture, etching, architecture. Despite the laws drawn from tradition, music contains one part miracle.

BG. The more so that the laws in question are truly empiric.

AH. We are wrong to think them intangible. Let us take for example the bi-thematic movement of the sonata. The treatises teach that this movement shows two themes confronting one another. But what no one says is that between the first and second theme there may be a multitude of others. Thus, in analysing the String Quartet, Op. 59, No. 1, of Beethoven, I find nine absolutely distinct themes. The difficulty is resolved by saying: there are the themes, the transitional episodes, the—

BG. The bridges.

AH. These are euphemisms. Why has not a given motif—under the pretext that it is the fifth or the sixth—the right to the noble name of theme? Because the sonata is said to be bi-thematic? It is absurd.

BG. Have you not given a masterly demonstration of your thesis in the second movement of your *Symphonie Liturgique*? You have sought—I have it from your own mouth—a development without doubling back or jointures, a melodic line which, starting from initial point A, strives to reach terminal point B by an uninterrupted trajectory. It is impossible to conceive of a purer and a more subtle form.

AH. You are too kind. True, I have sought above all a melodic line, which should be ample, generous, free-flowing, and not the laboured juxtaposition of little fragments which jar on one another. The larger melodic flow in no way excludes punctuation in the discourse; that is the touchstone in successful works;

we find it in all the masters. Nevertheless, exactly what a melody must be has been discussed and is still discussed. Criticism has denied the melodic gift at one time or another to Bach, Mozart, Beethoven, Schumann, Wagner, Gounod, Debussy. The grand word, when confronting a new work, is to say, 'It has no melody!' Figures like Pougin, Oscar Commettant, Fétis, Scudo, Hanslick, and a host of others, have admitted nothing as melody except motifs under formulas as simple and banal as possible: arpeggios (called 'noodles' in the professional jargon), or waltz rhythms (called 'rhyme and little dolls'). As soon as these same motifs are discovered to be accompanied by further melodies, that is, polyphonically accompanied, they lose quality and the right to the name in the eyes of these narrow-minded censors. How surprising to find this point of view in a Stravinsky in his *Poetics of Music*: 'At a time when Beethoven bequeathed the riches due in part to *this denial of the melodic gift*, another composer, whose merits never equalled those of the master of Bonn, was sowing to the winds, with tireless profusion, magnificent melodies of the rarest quality, distributing them as *freely* as he had received them, without a thought for recognition or credit for having begotten them.' And further on we read: 'Bellini had precisely what Beethoven lacked.' If this point of view appears to many to be somewhat paradoxical, they will the more appreciate the following statement: 'I *begin* to think, along with the great public, that melody must retain its place at the top of the hierarchy of the elements which compose music.'

I conceive the highest of melodic forms to be like the rainbow, which mounts and re-descends without one's being able to say at any one moment: 'Here, you see, it has returned to fragment B, there to fragment A'—all things which, besides, belong to the realm of craftsmanship and are of interest only to students. Listeners must be able to let themselves be carried along by melodic lines or rhythmic values, without concern for other matters.

BG. When Bach composed his Chorale No. 45, in E flat, 'O man, weep for your sins,' he did not cease to invent, on the very flexible plan of the melody.

AH. He embellished on a predetermined theme what has been called a major variation. Beethoven did the same, on a wretched little waltz by Diabelli, which inspired him to thirty-two variations, some of which have no connection in value or proportion with the original motif.

BG. No more connection than there is in content between the pebble which falls into the water and the concentric wave determined by its fall. We touch here on the problem of creative originality, the laws for which are certainly most difficult to identify.

AH. It is impossible. Such and such a harmony, a melodic line, a modulation, a rhythm, used by Peter, awakes no echo. Paul takes them up almost literally, and from the manner of his presentation, these same elements become the substance of his originality, the signature of his talent.

BG. Where precisely does the gift of musical invention lie? Is it in the elaboration of new harmonies? The thesis of the great critic Emile Vuillermoz was that the indicator of originality resides in the gift of harmonic renewal. He expressed this in a charming sentence: 'A fresh harmony is a bud that blossoms on the stem of eternal music.'

AH. Very well said, but observe the impasse we are driven to by such a formula. If Vuillermoz is right, we are forced to say that there can be no more great composers, for all the harmonic superimpositions have been used by now.

Absolute originality does not exist. Despite the remarkable novelty of his contributions, Debussy had his predecessors; for example, certain of Liszt's last pieces for piano are not so far from Debussy's *Préludes*. Before our Claude-Achille, the great Richard had pushed harmonic invention very far. Another Richard, contemporary of Debussy, author of *Elektra*, uncovered treasures in the realm of harmony. Moussorgsky, with his highly original instinct, had prospected in an area which Debussy boldly exploited. Thus Debussy himself did not suddenly leap forth from a vacuum. But his works have such a personal flavour that they unquestionably reflect a powerful genius and have revolutionized the musical world.

BG. The composer, then, works with the known and the unknown. He knows his profession, but he must create his own models. You have made allowance for both craft and inspiration, or, if one prefers, for divination–that groping in the darkness which, by the light of work, brightens only little by little.

AH. Let us detach a fragment of the *Martyrdom of Saint Sebastian*–the appearance of the Good Shepherd. There one finds some bars which give the listener the irresistible feeling of the invention of genius. To the technician, it is purely and simply a linking of tonic and dominant. Used in a certain manner, the simplest means are the most effective. The problem is to find many such!

BG. Claudel has said: 'The words I use are those of every day, and yet you tell me that you do not recognize them.' Does not all artistic creation consist in the uncommon use of ordinary materials?

AH. The poets are sometimes right.

CHAPTER 8

How I Work

*

The true artist always remains half
unaware of himself while he is
creating.

ANDRÉ GIDE

A H . How do I work? Am I able to define my methods? I am
not at all sure. To reply at all successfully, one would need the
ability to describe what takes place solely in the brain, to pierce
the wall behind which things are being acted out. Musical composition is the most mysterious of all the arts. One may learn by
watching a painter or sculptor at work. Many men of letters
dictate their books, working thus before witnesses. But the
moment a musician conceives a symphony, the instant he begins
composing, he is alone and in darkness. He must bring his score
to full completion before he can hear it. The painter and sculptor,
as I have already remarked, can compare their designs while
they are in the process of creation. You may see them step back,
judge, take up the brush or the chisel and correct a faulty detail.
But we musicians—impossible to verify before the audition;
when we wish to rectify, it is already too late!
B G . Therefore the most ardent of your disciples would learn
nothing by watching you compose?
A H . Nothing, I fear, except when I come to the orchestration.

He might, conceivably, be of aid to me, as the painter's students once upon a time sketched fragments of the whole, under the master's direction. Composition in music, the conception of the work, is a secret operation, mysterious and untransmittable. With the best good faith in the world, how explain the creative process?

I frequently compare a symphony or a sonata with a novel in which the themes are the characters. After we have made their acquaintance, we follow their evolution, the unfolding of their psychology. Their individual features linger with us as if present. Some of these characters arouse feelings of sympathy, others repel us. They are set off against one another or they join hands; they make love, they marry or they fight.

Or, if you prefer, take a comparison from architecture: imagine an edifice under construction, the general plan of which is first perceived but vaguely, and then progressively dawns upon the mind.

Like all the arts, we have rules which we have learned, and which have come down to us from the masters. But over and beyond the studied, consciously willed, inherited 'craft' of the profession, there remains a kind of compulsion for which we are not, so to speak, responsible. It is a drive from our subconscious which resists explanation.

B G. Now you find yourself midway between Berlioz–to whom an obliging god dictated his most sublime melodies–and a Stravinsky–under an objective control which overlooks no fragment of his work.

A H. To be as frank as possible, a great share of my work eludes my conscious will. To write music is to raise a ladder without a wall to lean it against. There is no scaffolding: the building under construction is held in balance only by the miracle of a kind of internal logic, an innate sense of proportion. I am at once the architect and the spectator of my own work: I work and I judge. When an unforeseen obstacle arrests me, I leave my construction and sit in the seat of the listener, saying to myself: 'After having heard the foregoing, what shall I hope for that will give me, if not the thrill of genius, at least the impression of success? What, logically, must happen to give me satisfaction?' And I try to find the next step, not the banal formula which would occur to everyone, but, on the contrary, an element of freshness, a rebound of interest. Step by step, following this method, my score is accomplished.

BG. Then one fine day, at an orchestral rehearsal, you hear for the first time the symphony which you have created in imagination. Do you ever experience great surprise when you confront the dream realized?

AH. The surprise is usually the evidence of insecurity, the fact of a musician who knows his profession only too badly. A composer worthy of the name must have foreseen everything. In that case, he is satisfied to verify by the ear what his brain has conceived. If I could profit by the painter's advantages, I should have an orchestra at my disposal to play my rough drafts in succession. That would be my way of stepping back to view my work. Unfortunately, this is not possible. I must wait for the general rehearsal. By that time, the orchestral personnel is set, the parts are copied, and any serious revision involves considerable labour. One must be satisfied with correcting errors in the copy. I am well aware that certain publishers will agree after the first edition to reprint whole pages; but, as you may suppose, these are not too numerous. Otherwise, one must learn to accept the risks.

The most appropriate comparison seems to me to be that of the shipbuilder who at the moment of launching risks seeing his vessel capsize. Fortunately the accident in music is not quite so evident. Many modern scores float upside-down; but very few people notice it.

*

BG. So then, I watch you compose, and yet what I want so much to grasp eludes me: how a theme comes before the world, the blossoming of a harmony, the elaboration of a plan. The work once achieved, are you able to relive the steps of your labour, the obstacles overcome, the moments of despair and the moments of grace? Can you describe after the event the process of a given creation?

AH. Only with great difficulty. The memory of anguishes and successes is quickly blurred. The child is born: one thinks then only of the future.

BG. Without too much apprehension?

AH. Mothers have none, they say.

BG. A man's point of view!

AH. No; all is forgotten, and first of all the bad moments.

BG. Does the final version which you settle on wipe out the memory of those which you almost adopted?

AH. Yes and no. When all is finished, I experience two quite distinct impressions. Either I say to myself: 'It didn't come off. If I begin all over again, I shall do everything quite differently.' Or I admit to myself, 'It's not bad. The progression of ideas is natural. There is no other solution.' But that is a personal opinion. I can describe the process of composition from a very subjective angle only. This must vary with musicians. Thus I should have no idea how Jacques Ibert might work.

BG. Even though you collaborated with him on the score for *L'Aiglon*.

AH. Or Darius Milhaud.

BG. Even though you were fellow-students at the Conservatory.

AH. As for the masters of the past, I can even less imagine their methods. Of my own work I know only the exterior, the rudiments. I forget all that others ask me to remember. For example, when the first performance of my *Symphony for Strings* occurred in Zürich, the organizers asked me to supply them with some recollections on the composition of this work. 'Tell us how the idea came to you.'

I could recall only the vaguest circumstances. My sole precise memory was thermal in nature: it was very cold at the time that I composed this symphony, and since it was impossible to build a fire in my studio, I was freezing. Evidently, there was no connection between this discomfort and the conception of my work.

BG. Just the same, how valuable it would be to invent a kind of film which would record for posterity the principal phases of the conception and realization of a musical masterpiece–a kind of reporting which, to be perfect, would require a camera in the the brain and not just in the composer's study.

AH. Often I have asked myself: 'How did Wagner compose?' His literary output is considerable, but he reveals nothing in it which touches at all closely on musical composition. He speaks endlessly about the elaboration of his poems, but of his hesitations, his moments of good fortune, his methods as a musician we know nothing.

BG. I should like to pass a summer in your company, leaving you to compose at your pleasure during the day, then in the evening to question you, pen in hand. I think that thus, while your memories were fresh, we might record the film of a day's work.

AH. At the moment, indeed, I have often said to myself: 'What a lot of interesting things I might entrust to someone on the subject of this opera! I shall give them to the journalists who interview me.' But, being too lazy to keep notes, I forget them, and when I am asked to remember, all is flown! Besides, let me tell you that if–by accident–you found yourself at my side when I was at work, my first thought would be to get rid of you, because at the very thought of being watched or listened to as I work, I freeze, my imagination dries up. That's why, indeed, I live quite alone, like a bear. When you might want to come to me in the evening and say, 'Well, cher Maître, what have you accomplished today? Are you satisfied with your work?' I should treat you as I would those ladies who pose this embarrassing query: 'Cher Maître, what are you producing for us next year?' I should degenerate at once into a regrettable rudeness!

BG. You do not like to analyse a work in the course of composition?

AH. I cannot: I am completely obsessed with my day's work. If it has gone badly, it is disagreeable for me to mention it. If it has gone well, I cherish to myself the momentary satisfaction and say: 'This evening, it's not too bad; but tomorrow, who knows, it may be necessary to start all over again.' I have the habit of reviewing the day's work each evening before retiring. Indeed, it is an excellent thing to practise an examination of one's conscience.

BG. Well then, I shall put questions for one simple purpose only, that of understanding an experience and of collecting documentation.

AH. Even so, what shall I say to you? With the best intention in the world, I should confide in you that here I changed a bass, that there I reworked three bars, that in another place this motif aroused the greatest hopes, and that suddenly I understood that it was absolutely foreign to the work I had in mind. I should say to you: 'This was too long, that was too short—' things without interest. Some of my colleagues may be much more lucid and gifted at describing what they mean to create. Unfortunately, I do not belong to that superior species!

*

BG. At the moment when your work begins to take form, no doubt I might share in your future projects?

AH. Perhaps, but it is not certain. Suppose I had in mind the project of composing a symphony. First of all, I experience great difficulty in determining the frame for my work. To me, a symphonic work must be built logically, without the possibility of interjecting the slightest anecdotal element between its different parts. I repeat: one must give the impression of a composition in which all is linked, the image of a predetermined structure. It has been said that architecture is frozen music. I should rather say that it is a geometry in time. Here, as elsewhere, one must be very exacting, so as to achieve an absolute equilibrium. If certain composers were the architects of their own houses, or builders of their own motor-cars, they would long ago have been reduced to rubbish!

BG. Will you pursue your comparison between the different arts?

AH. That seems natural enough. Of course, I am aware of differences in detail. For instance, we know that in painting the subject does not count; nevertheless, the boredom that accompanies a great exhibition may be compared to that from certain sonatas. Again, I insist, painters have certain undeniable advantages over us. I often say with a touch of envy to such as I know: 'What luck you have! Always your model before your eyes! Whether it's your three tedious apples that have bored us since Cézanne, or an ugly nude, or one of those harlequins who have plastered our walls for fifty years now—they are objects which you have seen and reproduce all day long, with more or less of personal emphasis.'

BG. No doubt they will answer that a painter worthy of the name is not looking for resemblances—for, in that case, photography would be superior to painting—but, on the contrary, for a certain distortion of reality, by which their talent is asserted.

AH. Look at the humorous magazines. The painter says to a lady: 'Madam, I shall paint your portrait,' and then he shows her three triangles, a cube and two discs, and assures her, 'That's the way I see you.'

BG. We could find less burlesque examples: Manet before a landscape or Monet painting the white waterlilies of Giverny.

Did not the genius of these two painters lie in their making a fairyland of reality, in creating perspectives which our layman's mundane eyes would never discover?

A H. It is what the psychoanalysts call 'sublimation'. From a commonplace bouquet of flowers, a cypress, a Van Gogh creates fireworks. But let us not enter too far into this domain, and let us not intolerantly misjudge that faithfulness to the model which certain contemporary painters consider ridiculous and outmoded. Such conceptions end up in those little *graffiti* found in public places, or which very young children draw on the margins of their notebooks. I do not believe in the naivety of sly old fellows of sixty years, or their alleged candour. Did I not see this kind of sketch described in the preface of a recent catalogue as 'auto-representations concealing perspectives of the ego?' Farther on we learn that Mr. X 'does not paint in the sense assigned to this act by the miserable contemporary hacks: he thinks out loud on the canvas . . .' If composers could think out loud on paper at thirty paces, that would singularly facilitate their work.

*

B G. A moment ago you used a dangerous word.

A H. And what was that?

B G. Facility. If you admit to working with facility, you suggest to the public that you have no merit. If you say you lack facility, they assume that you are not gifted.

A H. From a purely personal point of view, I should reply that I admire and envy composers like Milhaud and Hindemith, endowed with such facility that they write in a continuous out-pouring. It is true that Georges Auric has a very pertinent discrimination here: 'There are (he says) composers who write difficult music with ease, and others who write a facile music with difficulty.' As far as I am concerned, symphonic works give me much trouble: they demand an effort at sustained reflection. On the contrary, as soon as I can refer to a literary or visual pretext, my work becomes much easier. My dream would have been to compose nothing but operas: but that would have been labour lost in an age when the lyric theatre is on the way to disappearing.

BG. There is still film music.

AH. I have practised that for various reasons. There the work was relatively easy, for I possess the necessary technique to write an orchestral score swiftly. Besides, the subject is supplied by the picture, which immediately suggests to me a musical translation.

BG. Are you one of those composers of whom it is commonly said that they have their heads full of music all day long, whose brains automatically transform everything fed into them, visual, tactual, olfactory, into sound? Messiaen declares that the sight of a grotto with its stalactites immediately takes in him the form of a very special musical resonance.

AH. Simple question of habit. When the scenario of a ballet or a film is submitted to me, even if I feel that the project will never be realized, I very quickly imagine the appropriate music for such and such a passage. In Messiaen I see very clearly the musical reflection of stalactites: a succession of fourths, perfect or augmented, tumbling down or mounting again in pyramids, from low to high, in a ladder of sound.

BG. In the absence of some imaginative provocation, is your brain besieged by a perpetual symphony?

AH. No, Heaven be praised! Actually I proceed as follows.

I first seek the contour, the general aspect of the work. Let us say, for example, that I see taking form a sort of palace in a very opaque fog. Reflection progressively dissipates this fog and permits me to see a bit more clearly into it. Sometimes a beam of sunlight appears to illuminate a wing of the palace as it grows: this fragment then becomes my model. When this phenomenon spreads, I begin my search for my materials for construction. I prospect in my notebooks.

BG. You take notes?

AH. Gédalge gave me that habit. When a motif, a rhythm, an entire phrase comes to me, I jot it down. You know Beethoven's notebooks? Without being so presumptuous as to suggest a comparison, I admit that I proceed in the same way, and I recommend it to my pupils. So I check my notebooks of sketches in the hope of uncovering there some melodic design, a rhythmic plan, or some sequence of chords susceptible of being useful. Sometimes I think I have found what I am looking for, and I set to work. Often I start off on a false scent. Then, like a ragman, I take up my basket and set forth in quest of more appropriate fragments. I try again. I permit a melodic line to ripen, I prospect the different paths it opens to me. What disillusionment! One needs the courage to start again three, four, five times. Such, for those who ask, is the definition I have given of talent: 'The courage to begin again.' Sometimes, a very secondary element will yield the key to the problem. This rhythm or this motif, which had seemed banal to me, I suddenly perceive in its true light, it interests me passionately, and I will not abandon it for an instant.

BG. The lady you follow in the street you suddenly see as a deceptive skeleton.

In this elaboration of your work, does the tonal design play a major role? For Vincent d'Indy this plan played a determining role.

AH. To me, the 'tonal design' is an abstraction. I do not even understand what it means. I have had numerous friendly debates with d'Indy himself on this topic. I told him at the time that to me the dogma of tonality seemed an entirely outmoded notion. As well require a contemporary dramatist to observe the unity of place of the classical tragedy, which so many masterpieces cheerfully ignore! What gives unity to a piece of music is the totality of melodic and rhythmic relationships, elements much more powerful to affect the listener's spirit than the ties of tonality. Not everyone has 'absolute pitch'.

BG. It appears that Franck set down the tonal plan for his work at the top of his manuscript for his Symphony. It is said that he had decided upon it before having written a single note or jotted down the least theme.

AH. It is a technique completely foreign to me, though I find it absolutely legitimate if the work benefits by it.

BG. Imagine a painter's saying to himself before his virgin canvas: 'I shall compose a picture in which there will be red, yellow and green,' before he even knows what he is going to paint, or whether the development of his design would necessitate the use of these colours.

AH. Conceivably a painter, might say to himself: 'I am going to compose, not a true picture, but a study in red, yellow and green.' I believe we might find there one of the grounds for abstract painting. Musically, that escapes me: I cannot conceive of music fabricated by laws set up in advance. I am neither polytonalist, nor atonalist, nor a dodecaphonist. It is true, our contemporary musical material is based on a ladder of twelve chromatic sounds, but used with the same freedom as are the letters of the alphabet by the poet or the prismatic colours by the painter.

BG. In sum, then, you work out by instinct what others would do arbitrarily?

AH. I have endless admiration for Franck and d'Indy; their principles seem respectable to me, but not essential. Not that tonal music is true to life; but it seems to me that we can no longer tolerate this fetishism of tonality, which has been a burden on entire generations of musicians. Of much greater importance than tonal equilibrium are melodic and especially rhythmic balances. We should concern ourselves more with the architectural proportions, or, to borrow a literary comparison, the degrees of importance bestowed on this character as set off against that one. To transpose that into the language of music: here a theme A, of such and such a character, is followed by a theme B, which completes it or contrasts with it. The development of the first theme might require sixty bars, that of the second theme, eighty.

*

BG. You work a great deal, then?

AH. And very painfully, believe me!

BG. Would you describe for us one of your working days? You are composing a symphony.

AH. To be fruitful, a working day must not permit of any obligation or possibility of interruption. I am shut up in my studio, I try not to hear the doorbell or the telephone. Anyone who watched me without my seeing him would undoubtedly get the impression of a man on a holiday. I come and go, I take a book from a shelf, I re-read a favourite passage, I open a score. I offer, indeed, the picture of a man completely at leisure.

Nevertheless, I am unable to apply myself definitely to reading or to any other distraction, because I discover within me an urge for expression trying to seek the light of day.[1] Sometimes the day and night pass without my writing a note. Or I take a pencil and try to recover the points of departure which I had thought I had found and have lost. I am like a steam engine: I need to be stoked up, it takes me a long time to get ready for

[1] If this theme or that idea surges into the musician's mind during his sleep or as he walks, is that so astonishing? He sleeps. But nature is at work within him in deep secrecy, below his conscious mind; and without his knowledge and for his benefit, nature is taking pains to explore unhoped-for resources. It is at just such moments, when he seems side-tracked, that all sorts of forms are born within him, plans and schemes called up from his previous researches, by the desire which lies sleeping within him, the persistent need for invention which is his own, the power to conceive which is his own, and which involves him in a state of incessant and hidden activity. (*Music and the Interior Life*, Joseph Samson.) *Author's note.*

genuine work. If I relax for the duration of a month, I need days or weeks to get the machine in motion. This getting started becomes more and more painful with age. Nevertheless, the motor runs true only directly in gear.

I am a very conscientious man; there lies my misfortune. Naturally, all this has to do with a serious work, for example, the composition of a symphony. If it is a matter of film music, then it suffices to see the projection and to set to work; the visual image is quite fresh before my eyes. The more recent the film is in memory, the more my work is facilitated: the important thing is to transcribe the still lively impressions without delay.

BG. The whole difference between the drafting of an article and the composing of a novel. To come back to symphonic composition, let me ask you two questions to satisfy my curiosity: first, do you work at the piano?

AH. I do not play the piano well: therefore, I am incapable of summoning the muse by these brilliant musical runs, these lyric arpeggios, to which she is so susceptible. I am satisfied to use the piano to 'verify' what I have written, and to put myself back on the track from one day to the next: I warm up on the piano, which plays also the role of an aid to memory. The musical sound stimulates me up to the moment when–as when one suddenly hears the water begin to boil–something vaguely quivers within me.

BG. What do you think of composers who work exclusively at the piano?

AH. That has no importance. Nothing counts in this realm except to attain the goal one has set for himself. Stravinsky always works at the piano, because he feels the need of the constant reality of the actual sound. In certain cases, the danger of letting one's fingers run over the keys is that of falling into routine figuration and into the ease of improvisation.

BG. Another question: the place where you compose, the atmosphere surrounding you–are they of great importance?

A H . None at all. I have to have absolute solitude: no one must be able to see me or hear me when I am composing. I have a sort of elephantine modesty! If I know that anyone can enter the room where I am working, all is lost. This will explain why I rarely answer the telephone and why my door remains closed when the doorbell persists. One is often disturbed and often disappointed. Here is what the visitor-type is: 'I am not disturbing you? I'll stay only a moment.' And two hours later: 'I do not wish to disturb you, I'll telephone you to arrange a meeting.'

In contrast, street noises are anonymous, and, in some degree stimulating. I am in the centre of the noise, like a leaf in the forest, totally concealed, so well so that no one notices it further. The passing of cars masks human noises, radios, pianos, barking dogs, children shouting, and the rest.

All seasons are equally favourable to me—or unfavourable. If you want to know everything, I shall tell you that I work better in a small room than in a large, because it seems to me that the personal 'fluid'—this would delight Berlioz—more quickly saturates a small room. One senses an agreeable impression of concentration. So many manias, but sincere ones.

B G . It's the life of a hermit!

A H . When I am actually at work, I allow myself very few distractions during the day. In the evening I go to the cinema or to the home of some friends. As soon as the composition, strictly speaking, is completed and the orchestration is begun, there is nothing left but the applying of professional know-how—which is as pleasant as painting. The sole difficulty in my profession is—to conceive.

B G . As you grope in the darkness, do you sometimes have the grace of an illumination?

A H . A rational composer finds the golden mean between prose and poetry, between work and what you like to call inspiration. We must not delude ourselves about it, but know how to welcome it when it comes.

BG. Could you describe one of these happy moments?

AH. Yes; it is disappointing. I am a worrier, and when I am bathing in the joy of discovery, my guardian angel whispers in my ear: 'It is not possible. It is a reminiscence – or a happy dream. It will all collapse. These eight pages gave me so much trouble; here, abruptly, are sixteen at one stroke!' Picture the gold seeker: he thumps away with his pick, he is in a sweat, he can do no more, he will never find anything. And, suddenly, there is the nugget; he can't believe his eyes. There are, however, illustrious precedents: Wagner, writing to Mathilde Wesendonck: 'My child, the first act of *Tristan* is something unbelievable!' Which obviously means, of unbelievable beauty: and how right he was! In the presence of such enthusiasms let us be lenient. Let us be the same for the artist who, though he has not written the first act of *Tristan*, loves and admires what he has done. Remember that it is his sole excuse!

BG. What can be finer in the world than a man sincerely astonished at what he has achieved?

AH. Sometimes a melodic idea comes to one with such finality of form that one has difficulty getting it down. The result is a certain discomfort: 'Is it a windfall, a discovery?' It takes real courage then not to touch further what one has just written.

BG. So, this frightful toil does permit of its fine moments?

AH. If we had to toil without ceasing, workers would be rare, believe me. Let us allow certain illusions to live!

BG. Berlioz was right!

AH. So long as he did not take the exception for the rule. It takes a lot of work to earn this happy relaxation, much lucidity to arrive at no longer noticing what surrounds us, much patience and immobility to capture one of these brief voyages into the land of living music.

CHAPTER 9

How I Judge Myself

*

The fact for the true artist is not to take
delight in what he has done, but to
compare it sadly with what he would
wish to have done.

COURTELINE

BG. From an artist the public expects much more than a work.
It hopes for a judgement brought to bear on this work by the
one who made it. With this in mind, it frequently interrogates
creators, though it is often disappointed in its expectations. Very
often, the creators refuse to answer, or they answer aside from
the question. A sincere conviction is disguised under the mask of
expediency. During their own lifetime a legend is built.

To serve as the exception which tests the rule, will you give us
a sincere and objective opinion on yourself and your work?

AH. You ask me to judge myself? That is exceedingly difficult
and complex. I am what is called in the language of passports a
'double national', that is, a mixture of French and Swiss.

Born in Le Havre of Swiss parents, I have lived the greater
part of my life in France, pursued my studies there as if I had
been French, yet carried deep within me a germ, a Swiss atavism,
what Milhaud called 'my Helvetian sensitiveness'.

What do I owe to Switzerland? No doubt the Protestant

tradition, great difficulty in deluding myself about the value of what I do, a naive sense of integrity, a familiarity with the Bible–very disparate elements.

What do I owe to Le Havre? My childhood years, and the passion of those happy years–the sea. I loved the ships, especially the sailing vessels. I knew the different models of ships by their names, and the parts of their gear–the square-rigged three-masted ones, the brigs, the schooners. The sea had a profound influence, and enlarged the horizon of my childhood. In addition to the sea, I must not forget my favourite sports, foot-racing, swimming, football, rugby.

I began to write music at Le Havre. Even before I learned anything I had in me a vague desire to compose. As a small child I drafted imaginary reviews for my future work: 'In 1903 Arthur Honegger wrote his famous overture.' A fixed idea, I believe, is the lodestone for a whole careeer. However, this impulse blossomed in surroundings which were scarcely propitious. My family was not what is called a family of musicians, even though the art was practised in it; and at the time of my youth, Le Havre was one of the least musical cities imaginable: a few performances of opera at the theatre; from time to time, a concert by a virtuoso on tour. In this way I heard for the first time Enesco, Sarasate, Ysaÿe and Pugno, the Cortot-Thibaud-Casals trio, the admirable Capet Quartet playing before some twenty people. My schoolmates at the lycée, like their parents, had no thought for anything but commerce and business; most of them did not even suspect the existence of music. One of them one day, hearing me pronounce the name of Mozart, reproached me sternly: 'You mean Mansart.'

'No, Mozart.'

'But no, Mansart, the inventor of the mansard roof.' Thus he knew Mansart for one of his humblest motifs only (there were some mansard roofs at the lycée), and was blatantly ignorant of the name of Wolfgang Amadeus Mozart!

We had music in class once a week. At the distribution of prizes we sang *Love and Spring* by Waldteufel—a little piece with strangely inappropriate words for children of eight or ten, but beautiful music ennobles everything, does it not?

> On délire!
> On désire,
> On soupire,
> La nuit et le jour!
> L'innocente
> Est tremblante,
> Mon coeur chante:
> C'est l'amour![1]

*

I began by being self-taught.

After having learned the rudiments of the scale, I read Beethoven's sonatas, which led me to discover the tonal system. The idea of writing some sonatas myself came quite naturally to me. I forced my poor mother to play my concoctions at sight. Later, I was given a teacher of harmony. I worked slowly, without any great facility or great enthusiasm for a science which seemed rather arbitrary to me.

Not satisfied with writing sonatas, I wanted to compose operas. I had already perpetrated two at a time when I scarcely knew how to write the signatures. I had done the text, the music, and the binding! It was the binding that gave me the most trouble!

---

[1] Impossible to translate exactly in verse, but we might try something like this:

We are on fire	Sweet young things
With desire	Are trembling strings,
With sighs expire	And my heart sings:
Night and day!	Give love its way. *Translator's note.*

After I discovered the libretto of *Esmeralda* which Victor Hugo had written for Mlle Bertin, I did not hesitate to enter into competition with this poet, whose glory, rather than dazzling me, set me bravely to work. I gave it up in the midst of the second act, finding my verses rather flat, and returned to my sonatas.

During that period I took up the violin and, like the masters, wrote my sonatas in groups of six, at least. Then, in honour of my friend Georges Tobler, today director of the French Bank of Rio de la Plata in Argentina, then a budding violinist, I composed some sonatas for two violins and piano.

All this was immature, even childish, no doubt. In consequence of which there was a serious set-back, which came to light when I entered the Conservatory, in the class under Gédalge —and that in spite of a period of two years at the conservatory of Zürich. The director of the latter institution, Friedrich Hegar, friend of Brahms, became interested in me, and influenced my father to let me enter on the uncertain career of composer. My father's approval was heroic—this I say without joking— because my father had four children, and yet he consented to subsidize my needs for years, perhaps for my lifetime.

B G . Would you tell us now what you owe to France?

A H . Le Havre is in France, I believe, and I think I have said at length what I owe to Le Havre. The rest I owe to France: intellectual illumination, my musical and spiritual refining.

I arrived in Paris at the age of nineteen, nourished on the classics and the romantics, enamoured of Richard Strauss and Max Reger, the last completely unknown in Paris. In contrast I found, not that school, but the Debussyites in full bloom; I was introduced to d'Indy and to Fauré. I gave much time to fathoming the character of Fauré, whom I took for a long time to be a musician of the salons. Once past this period, I surrendered with delight to his example. Debussy and Fauré made a very useful counterbalance, in my aesthetics and my feeling, to the classics and Wagner.

B G . While we are on the subject of influences—

A H . Let us note the influence of Stravinsky and Schoenberg, but let us not forget that of my classmate, Darius Milhaud. He worked, acted, spoke, with an assurance, a gift for invention, and a daring which dazzled the timid little provincial! He introduced me right and left, he revealed composers to me whom I had not suspected—Magnard, Séverac— and, what is more, was very fond of me. I returned it fully. At the same time, his influence and our friendship left us our complete independence. He became a fervent advocate of Satie, and I, in turn, never cried: 'Down with Wagner!'

There is one other person whom I do not mention when I am asked about influences, but a man who contributed more to my career than certain masters. I mean Fernand Ochsé, musician, painter, literary figure, stage designer, who has had the most happy influence on my development. He was an incomparable friend to me, whose memory I cherish in profound gratitude. His disappearance during the terrible days of the Occupation remains one of the deepest sorrows of my life. Since that time, I have never heard one of my new works without wondering: 'What would Fernand have thought of it?'

*

B G . We know who are your gods, we are acquainted with your two fatherlands—one of origin, one of adoption. We should like to know what has been your central ambition as a composer.

A H . My inclination and my effort have always been to write music which would be comprehensible to the great mass of listeners and at the same time sufficiently free of banality to interest genuine music lovers.

B G . An art at once popular and personal.

A H . Especially in the scores which have generously been labelled 'great frescoes' have I followed this double goal, endeavouring to find a design as clean-cut as possible, without surrendering the enrichment of the musical substance, harmonic or contrapuntal. My rule as artist is softened in my advice to my students: 'If your melodic or rhythmic design is precise and clear and commands the attention of the ear, the accompanying dissonances will never frighten the listener. What discourages him is to wallow in a bog of sound from which no shore is visible and in which he swiftly sinks. It is then that he grows bored and will no longer listen.' One may, one must, speak to the great public without concessions, but also without obscurity. This is why a fair number of my works have reached the ear of the public: I am thinking of *King David*, *Judith*, *The Dance of the Dead*, *Joan of Arc at the Stake*.

B G . Since Stravinsky has turned his back on his 'first manner', and Falla is dead, composers who unite this twofold preference are not numerous; namely, to be themselves and to speak to others besides themselves.

A H . Some are afraid of falling into banality; they are afraid to be simple, they dread the idea that they are not revolutionizing the world at every new work. It's a curious obsession, this idea of perpetual revolution. An incessant springtide of newness would soon lead to the exhaustion of musical matter. I always remember one of Fauré's great sayings: 'Do not try to be a genius in every bar.' And yet he himself was just that!

B G . These statements of principles seem to carry more importance than *a posteriori* pronouncements. Once you answered your friend Cocteau as follows, which seems capital to me: 'If I still participate in a state of things in their last stages, it is because it seems to me indispensable that, to progress, we must be solidly linked with what has preceded us. We must not break the tie with musical tradition. A branch separated from the trunk quickly dies. We must be the new player in the same old game, because to change the rules is to destroy the game and to throw it back to its starting point. Economy of means seems to me more difficult, but also more useful, than a too headstrong audacity. There is no profit in smashing the door which you might open.'

The second declaration–

AH. That word smells of the customs official and says nothing of value to me!

BG.–you made to Paul Landormy: 'I attach great importance to musical architecture, which I should never wish to see sacrificed to literary or pictorial obligations. I tend, perhaps too much so, to look for polyphonic complexity. My great model is Johann Sebastian Bach. I do not, like certain anti-impressionist musicians, seek a return to harmonic simplicity. On the contrary, I argue that we must make use of the harmonic resources created by the school preceding us, but in a different way, as a base for line and rhythm. Bach made use of the elements of tonal harmony, as I should wish to make use of modern harmonic superpositions. I am no worshipper of the fair-grounds or the music-hall, but, quite the opposite, of chamber music and symphonic music, and when they are at their most serious and most austere.'

Your pronouncements define more than a preference: they are a doctrine. You are linked with the masters, and yet you are a free man. You are already a classic without ever having been behind the times. Your language is new, but not arbitrary. You are tonal, atonal, polytonal, according to your own good pleasure, or as circumstances may require. You are a learned and original musician, yet you touch the popular feeling. You are of interest– a feeble word– to specialists, and you know how to move the soul of the people.

AH. This declaration is personal to you. I should gladly subscribe to it if I felt that I could justify it. Have I been successful? I do not know. But I have tried. I have wanted to touch the two publics: the technicians and the multitude. At certain moments, it has seemed that I have achieved my goal; for example, when I heard the peasants of Jorat in Switzerland singing the Alleluias from *King David*.

BG. Remember, too, the first performance of *Joan of Arc at the Stake* at Orléans. The specialists were in the minority; the major part of the audience was anonymous. The sign of your success was that composers and musicologists could admire the skill with which you conducted the unfolding of the final chorus, and the people of Orléans could feel their eyes dim because they felt themselves, not in a concert hall, but, like the common folk of Rouen long ago, gathered around the stake of Joan of Arc, watching the Saint consumed 'like a flame in the heart of France'. Are there many composers of our time who can say as much?

AH. I am the last to be able to answer that question.

BG. I go on record at least that you do not answer in the negative.

*

BG. You have defined your aims, and I have commented on your success. There remains for our information the means you have employed.

AH. Of first importance in these means, I should place a concept of prosody—of setting words to music and music to words—which is somewhat peculiar to me. And I should add immediately a shocking thing: French composers appear not to recognize the plastic significance of the texts which they set to music. Here I share the doubts of Richard Strauss when he was composing *Salome*, following the text of Oscar Wilde: 'Why do the French sing differently from the way they speak? Is it atavism or tradition?' Upon which Romain Rolland advised him to study *Pelléas* carefully, which he considered to be the best example of good French words with music. Strauss bought the score, worked it over, and was astonished to discover 'that same indifference to delivery, which from the beginning has so surprised me in French music'.

For me, the problem arose in the same way. At the time I was composing the music for *Antigone*, on a violent and even brutal text, I sometimes said to myself: 'If I combine words and music for this text in the customary fashion, it will lose its character, its power. *Pelléas* is an exceptional case. Maeterlinck's monochrome poem actually suggests this monotonous repetition, this impassive syllabism, by the use of which the sub-Debussyites have dragged the lyric theatre to its death. In any case, Debussy's success cannot serve as a model for dramatic delivery.'

What I had to work out at all costs was the means whereby I might make others *understand* the lyric text: that, in my opinion, was the rule of the game in the realm of the lyric. French dramatic musicians show an exclusive concern for the melodic design and a quite subordinate care for the conformity of text and music. Hence the legend that in the lyric theatre one can never understand the singers. Now, ninety-nine times out of a hundred, it is not the singers' fault, but the fault of the composers.

I had, at all costs, to dissociate myself from this careless prosody, as from the Debussyite droning. Therefore I sought for the right stress, especially on the attacking consonants, finding myself in this respect in clear-cut opposition to traditional principles. In this I had the happiness to be supported by Claudel, whose doctrine I had hitherto not known. What is important in the word is not the vowel, but the consonant: it really plays the role of a locomotive, dragging the whole word behind it. In classical singing, in the world of the *bel canto*, the vowel is queen, because one can hold the sound as long as one wishes on A,E,I,O,U. In our time, and for a dramatic delivery, the consonants project the word into the hall, they make it resound. Each word contains its potential, its melodic line. The addition of a melodic line in opposition to its own paralyses its flight, and the word collapses on the floor of the stage. My personal rule is to respect the word's plasticity as a means of giving it its full power.

Take an example from *Antigone*. At one instance, Créon

violently interrupts the choir, crying out: 'Assez de sottises, vieillesse!' The conventional prosody suggests the following stress: 'Assez de sot*ti*ses, vieil*le*sse!' Try to project this phrase in anger, with this rhythm: the aggressive effect is immediately blunted. Respecting the dramatic situation and Créon's anger, I made it: 'Assez de *sottises vieil*lesse!' leaning on the roots of the words. The same for: 'L'homme est *i*nouï–l'homme *la*boure–l'homme *cha*sse.' I placed the stress on the downbeat.

This approach has been generally disapproved by composers and critics, but, to my great joy, singers, after they had raised their arms to the skies with 'Heavens, how complicated this music is!' came to me after the second rehearsal saying, 'You are right: when one has got the habit, one can no longer think of singing it otherwise.' My system helped them chiefly in sentences of rapid delivery, as well as in the high register.

B G. The public, without its knowledge, benefits by this method. Thus, in *Joan of Arc at the Stake*, when the choir begins in the last act: 'Louée soit notre *soeur* Jeanne, qui est *de*bout, pour *tou*jours, comme une *flamme*, au *mi*lieu de la *France*!', the audience is as much impressed by the stress which you have known how to give this sentence as by its melodic and harmonic beauty.

A H. This prosodic system is carried to its fullest in *Antigone*. I have used it elsewhere, however. When I have a text to set to music, I have the author read it to me, or, if he is a poor reader, I imagine the way a good actor would utter it, how he would place the major stresses. If two or three key words are given their full value in a sentence, the general sense is immediately made clear. To find myself in full accord with Claudel on this point was for me a powerful satisfaction. Claudel gave me the most precious support: the theory I was advocating was no longer a whim, a musician's trick, but the studied opinion of the greatest poet of our times. I can equally invoke the testimony of Paul Valéry, who likewise agreed with me. By applying these principles, I simply wanted to restore a native simplicity and ease to

French singing. Strictly speaking, I had not written a recitative, but melodies rapidly sung, so rapidly even that many thought they were not melodies. What is generally admired is the slow melody. Ask anyone to cite you a beautiful melody, and it will surely be marked *adagio*. And that is absurd. But to enumerate all the absurdities made sacred by custom would fill the shelves of a library.

*

B G. You have just commented on certain experiments of yours—why you undertook them, how you carried them out. Our curiosity is insatiable: we should like to know your personal judgement on some of your works. I accost the father of a family, surrounded by his daughters, and say point-blank: 'Which one seems to you the most beautiful?'

A H. Thank Heavens, I have a poor memory: I acknowledged my daughters at their birth, but I have since forgotten them! So, when I happen to meet one of them after a long absence, I look at her with a certain objectivity, and, as the case may be, say to myself: 'Well! She's not so bad!' or, on the contrary: 'That one—hmm!'

For me as for my colleagues, it is the scores most 'up to date' that show the most wrinkles. Certain lighter things, admissible in 1920, make a disastrous showing in 1951.

BG. The calmness of your judgement is what makes it precious to us.

AH. I wrote a certain number of works 'by sheer force'—that's the way to characterize especially formidable trials. I consider them somewhat as Beethovenian by-products. You will say: the poor man's Beethoven. Agreed; but they were nevertheless those that expressed my true nature. In this category I have a secret preference for certain pieces not always warmly appreciated: the Quartets, especially the first, because it exactly expressed the personality of the young man who wrote it in 1917. There are faults, slow passages, but I recognize myself in it as in a mirror. As a sample of better work I shall select my third Quartet, which marked a progress in conciseness and workmanship. Finally, I have a certain tender feeling for the *Lamento* in the *Dance of the Dead*, whose realization was not too far from the design I had in mind.

As to symphonies, I value in my *Symphonie Liturgique* the fact that it is very little indebted to traditional aesthetics. In my opinion, the following symphony, the *Deliciae Basiliensis*, marks a progress in craftsmanship, and contrasts well with what had gone before, and this is indispensable. As to the Fifth, which I have just heard, conducted by my friend Charles Münch, I am not yet sufficiently detached from it (it dates from the end of 1950) to judge it with complete objectivity. I have already pointed out a few errors, yet at the same time I do find one passage worthy–I shall not tell you which. Besides, the articles by your colleagues will enlighten us on this subject.

BG. *Joan of Arc at the Stake?*

AH. Claudel's contribution was so great that I hardly see myself as the real author, but as a humble collaborator.

BG. I know that *Antigone* is one of your favourite daughters.

AH. It is true that I attach some importance to it: it embodies my ambitions and my lyric efforts. Without shallow pride or false modesty, I believe that *Antigone* brought a little pebble to the lyric theatre. But this pebble has since fallen to the bottom of a pit and remained there.

BG. What is your reaction to hearing *King David*?

AH. That is one work which has succeeded in slipping into the famous 'repertory' of programmes. So when it's a question of finding a 'modern work' for a music festival, the planners decide on *King David*. The choral groups know it, also the orchestras: hence a minimum of rehearsals, economies, and a satisfied public. Those who are least satisfied–and I fully understand–

are the other composers, who have a completed score not yet played in public, and whose place I seem to keep on usurping.

The performance of *King David* arouses no very strong feelings in me. I listen with a certain boredom–and do not think I am being hypocritical in this opinion. I try on such occasions to pretend that I am a spectator among the others, and I endeavour to sort out the good qualities from the faults.

The principal defect in *King David* lies in the fact that a work originally conceived as a score to accompany a drama, as music for the stage, is today offered as an oratorio. I illustrated this drama as an engraver would illustrate the chapters of a book, with chapters in it of greater or less length. On the stage all proceeds quite naturally; but in a concert, there are too many brief passages in the first part, and that gives the impression of fragmentation.

B G . May we look at it in some detail?

A H . You want to know where I begin to grow bored? I can tell you precisely: at No. 6 of the first part. I open an eye at No. 8, because I wish to verify that it will this time, again, be played too fast. At the *Chorus of Prophets* and at the *Camp of the Israelites* I doze off peacefully. I awake at the words, 'The Eternal is my light.' *The Dance before the Ark*, despite certain details, gives me a kind of satisfaction, because there is a good sense of progress about its development. In the third part, my preference goes to the *Chorus of Penitence*. Candidly, proudly, I admit that the ending, the combination of the Chorus with the Alleluias, seems to me to accomplish in some degree what I had hoped for.

B G . What can you say of the *Pacific*? Everyone knows that you wanted to depict the starting of a locomotive, of the type Pacific 231, and then its course at full speed.

A H . That is in effect what is said, but such was not my purpose.

B G .—

A H . One should never go to useless trouble for the public–that is one of the basic laws of musical composition. So many,

many critics have so minutely described the onrush of my locomotive across the great spaces that it would be inhuman to disabuse them! One of them, confusing *Pacific* with the Pacific Ocean, even evoked the smells of the open sea. To tell the truth, in *Pacific* I was on the trail of a very abstract and quite ideal concept, by giving the impression of a mathematical acceleration of rhythm, while the movement itself slowed. Musically, I composed a sort of big, diversified chorale, strewn with counterpoint in the manner of J. S. Bach.

BG. But the title?

AH. I first called this piece *Mouvement Symphonique*. On reflection, I found that a bit colourless. Suddenly, a rather romantic idea crossed my mind, and when the work was finished, I wrote the title, *Pacific 231*, which indicates a locomotive for heavy loads and high speed (a type unfortunately disappeared, alas, and sacrificed to electric traction).

BG. Are you taking advantage of our credulity?

AH. No. I was making an experiment. I had composed, as you recall, three 'Symphonic Movements,' which were *Pacific 231*, *Rugby*, and, to conclude—

BG. *Mouvement Symphonique, No. 3*.

AH. As a matter of fact, I lacked an idea for the third. But you must know that as regards *Pacific* and *Rugby*, the press turned out to be very prolix. People of great talent wrote wonderful articles describing the driving-rods, the noise of the pistons, the grinding of the brakes, the oval balloon, the release of steam, the commotion of the front wheels, etc., etc. All these images gave birth to copious studies. But my poor *Symphonic Movement No. 3* paid dearly for its barren title: it barely harvested here and there a few evasive and polite lines. Moral:—but no, I have been a music critic myself, and I prefer not to speak ill of a profession which has fed me.

BG. What do you think of—

AH. Oh no! I am quite willing to answer a question, but not

an examination. Remember that an author goes to great pains to build his works. Spare him at least the drudgery of judging them.

BG. As you say: but on one condition.

AH. Which is?

BG. That you grant us the liberty of cherishing them.

CHAPTER 10

I Have Collaborated

*

Never collaborate!
OCTAVE MIRABEAU

W hen the composer of music wishes to step out of the realm of the symphony or the sonata, if he wants to undertake a dramatic work or simply write a melody, he has to seek the aid of a collaborator. Should this collaborator be a dead author? That is plain sailing, provided that one respects the rules set up for permission to make free use of the text. If it belongs to the public domain, then even the worst distortions do not invite penalties. Up and after the unlucky fellow who has been dead fifty years: he is at our mercy.

Collaborations among musicians are many and varied. Whether it be transcriber or poet (passing over the instrumentalist), choreographer or scenario-writer, they illustrate to what degree the composer is dependent on others. As a general rule, the collaborator's claims are in inverse proportion to his talent. Nothing is easier than to verify this statement in the domain of the cinema, where the musician is ranked with the poor relative.

If the stage-manager and the producer are cultivated gentlemen, and have some notion of what music is, it is relatively easy to arrive at an understanding. They give the musician confidence. But when such is not the case, the musician has to argue step by step the absurd fantasies they hope to impose on him. What weariness, and to no purpose, and all because the scenario-writer has unlimited power at his disposal.

There are better days, fortunately. A musician sometimes experiences the joy of contact with the most eminent artists of his time, poets or novelists. This is the reward for many a rebuff, and it most usefully feeds the springs of individual invention.

*

Through the intervention of a mutual friend, Henriette Charasson, I made the acquaintance of Apollinaire, for whom I had already set six poems to music, excerpts from his *Alcools*.

Apollinaire had returned from the front and had undergone head surgery as a consequence of a serious wound. Max Jacob said: 'He knows nothing of music, he likes no one but Schubert.' In this same Café Flore, which had become an existentialist hangout, I was introduced to Cocteau, who played an important role in the post-war musical world. We had some wonderfully fine evenings with him as the animator. They brought together painters–Fauconnet, Picasso, Dufy–men of letters–Giraudoux, Morand, Radiguet, Lucien Daudet–and musicians of the group known as *Les Six*, including Satie. When Cocteau's adaptation of *Antigone* was performed at the Atélier, I wrote a little score for the stage for oboe and harp. Later, this rapid and violent text incited me to compose my musical tragedy. Without being genuinely a musician, Cocteau served as a guide to many young folk. He stood for the general sense of a reaction against the pre-war aesthetic. Each one of us translated that in a different manner.

I was also allied with Max Jacob; he gave me the libretto of a

Sainte Alméenne which got buried in my papers. During the same period, I had a chance to become acquainted with Blaise Cendrars, whose extraordinary personality expressed itself in all spheres, and who authorized me to set to music some fragments of his beautiful poem, *Easter in New York*. I also met Paul Fort, who has entrusted so many poems to musicians, and the Belgian poet Paul Méral with whom I collaborated for the music of *Dit des Jeux du Monde*. Produced in December 1918 at the Vieux-Colombier under the direction of Jeanne Bathori, this work managed to arouse some excitement, but the very original costumes by Fauconnet unquestionably marked a date in the history of the theatre.

At the beginning of 1921, I received a letter from René Morax, who with his brother Jean had founded the Théâtre du Jorat, in the village of Mézières, a dozen kilometres above Lausanne. Every two years they put on there a series of performances. Morax asked me to write the score for a *King David* which he hoped to produce in May of the same year.

Without fully realizing the importance of the work which had been entrusted to me, I accepted with pleasure, since the subject perfectly suited my 'Biblical' tastes. I cherish among my best memories these performances and especially the preparation of this work. Happy period! Students, peasants, professionals, co-operated in the enjoyment. Three painters, Jean Morax, Cingria and Hugonnet, painted the scenery and the costumes. There were twenty-seven scenes, and we had chariots drawn by real horses! Success crowned our efforts. To facilitate the hearing of my score at the concert, Morax had the idea, often repeated since, of linking the rather brief passages by a text assigned to a solo narrator, whose task it was to summarize the action.

Two years later came *Judith* with Croiza and Alcover, with my faithful Paul Boepple again in the conductor's stand, he who had already produced *King David*. Following that came a light comedy, *La Belle de Moudon*, which we produced with the aid of

Moudon's brass band. During the Occupation, I wrote a short
score for *Charles the Bold*. I have never heard it.

For the production of André Gide's *Saul* I composed stage
music for a little ensemble placed below the floor of the stage at
the Vieux-Colombier; and some thirty years later, music for the
translation of *Hamlet*, which Jean-Louis Barrault played at the
opening of his theatre at Marigny.

*

This listing is becoming tedious, for I should need more than
one chapter to tell all I owe to different collaborators.

It was Madame Ida Rubenstein, incomparable interpreter and
patroness, who put me in touch with Saint-Georges de
Bouhélier, d'Annunzio and Claudel. As for Saint-Georges de
Bouhélier, it was again a question of theatre music designed for a
great spectacle at the Opéra; *L'Impératrice au Rocher* ('The
Empress of the Rock'), which was sumptuously produced with
scenery and costumes by Benoît. Nevertheless, Bouhélier was not
entirely satisfied. He particularly complained that the orgy scene
was lacking in nude women. We tried to persuade him to accept
the usual tradition of the subsidized theatre, but he was obstinate:
'I demand nude women!'

The staging was entrusted to the celebrated Sanine. To bring
the actors into the atmosphere of the orgy, he forced poor Mlle
Atoch to play all the music on a wretched rehearsal piano,
battered by generations of ballet performers. This was done amid
the greatest consternation. Then, calling off the whole thing,
Sanine exclaimed: 'You have heard that horrible music: it's a
disaster, a real disaster!'

It was true. My music had no success, and nevertheless Madame
Rubenstein asked me again to furnish the music for Gabriele
d'Annunzio's *Phaedra*, which she was about to play at the
Costanzi Theatre in Rome. My score was unfortunately

smothered by the hoots and boos of Fascist youth. They had been promised the presence of d'Annunzio, who did not come because he was, in fact, already a prisoner in his Vittoriale. The public boisterously expressed its disappointment at having uselessly collected a whole swarm of banners.

D'Annunzio had invited me to visit him at this estate where, looming from the midst of a garden, the whole front of a cruiser came into view. We climbed the gangway, which was guarded by a marine, arms at order. D'Annunzio took me to admire the magnificent view on Lake Garda, then he said: 'And now, to honour the musician who comes to visit the poet, we shall launch the seven notes of the scale into that infinity which has neither number nor limits. Fire!' A terrific explosion of cannon almost threw me flat. Do! Re! Mi! So we climbed the whole scale!

The next day he took me to the installation of the air base at Desenzano, then he conducted me to Milan. I have never seen him since.

His conversation was a display of fireworks, and one understood how this man of a predominantly unattractive physique had such success with women. He was understandably proud of his mastery of the French language. 'Most French writers,' he was fond of repeating, 'are satisfied with fifteen hundred words. I know fifteen thousand!'

I collaborated also with Romain Rolland for *Liluli*, and with Madam Elisabeth de Grammont on a ballet, *Roses de Métal* ('Silver Roses'), the orchestra for which was composed of four Bertrand dynaphones, the début of these sound-wave instruments. I had begun a kind of light comedy with Jacques Copeau, *The King, his Vizier, and his Physician*, which was never completed.

The Exhibition of 1937 having called for a certain number of *Displays of Water and Light* to be given on the Seine, I collaborated on a recreation of the *Thousand and One Nights* with Dr Mardrus, translator of that work.

As to Jean Giraudoux's *Sodom and Gomorrah*, my collaboration was limited to certain interpolations for a group of trombones. Giraudoux's death cut short our project for a 'grand opera' in the stately style, on a subject which had also been proposed to me by the charming René Kerdyck–*Alceste*. For a festival of the Hautes Etudes Commerciales, I wrote the music for a ballet on one of Sacha Guitry's ideas, *Un oiseau blanc s'est envolé* ('A white bird has taken flight'), for which Lifar arranged the choreography.

When the choir of Soleure (Switzerland) commissioned a work from me for its fiftieth anniversary celebration, I asked René Bizet to supply a text, and he gave me *Cris du Monde* ('Cries of the World'). Some of my friends have insinuated that I should have drafted the text and left to Bizet the task of composing the score. Though favourably received in Switzerland, its reception in Paris was indifferent. Some saw a communist work in it, others a reactionary hymn. Actually, in it I gave expression to the revolt of the individual against the crowd that crushes him–a timely subject.

In the lighter realm I worked with Willemetz: *Le Roi Pausole* (based on the text of Pierre Louys' *Les Aventures du Roi Pausole*) profited from the excellent interpretation of Dorville, René Koval, Pascali, Jacqueline Francell, among others, and ran for almost 500 performances. Later, with the collaboration of Jacques Ibert, it was *Les Petites Cardinal*, whose career was less happy. We worked together on the music of *L'Aiglon*, following the play by Rostand. *L'Aiglon* ('The Eaglet'), performed at Monte Carlo by Raoul Gunsbourg, then revived at the Opéra, was never again played, despite a considerable public success.

*

At the same period, I launched a project which Paul Valéry had already discussed with me some years earlier. This was *Amphion*, which Madame Rubenstein presented at the Opéra, and which was followed by *Sémiramis*. In *Amphion* I carried out a project which Valéry had previously entrusted to Debussy; a great honour, a heavy responsibility. Valéry explained in detail his intent in this work by means of a lecture which he gave at the Annales, and which appears in his *Pieces on Art*.

The failure of *Sémiramis* was amply compensated for by the joy of work accomplished at Valéry's side. He was not only a great poet but a charming man as well. At every moment he found the opportunity or the pretext to develop an idea with an extraordinary power of expression. Like all men of his era, he had been most impressed by Wagner's art, and it was always to Wagner that he referred when he spoke of music. Not knowing either the language or the discipline, he respected that art. Thus, in *Sémiramis*, after two scenes heavily laden with music, the heroine suddenly turns to speech. When I wanted to halt the music for the words, to give the text its full value, Valéry said half jokingly, half seriously, 'Run a little tremolo under it for me!' And the monologue lasted for seventeen minutes!

He submitted a fine project to me which, alas, we did not have the leisure to complete. This would have begun with a text in prose; then the prose would have been relaxed towards a more and more rhythmic poetry, which, in turn, would have given way to music at the precise moment when the power of words came to a halt.

I have not forgotten the personality of Ricciolo Canudo, apostle of the seventh art, the cinema. It was he who introduced me to Abel Gance, with whom I several times collaborated in my first experiences with film music. With Canudo I wrote, for the Swedish Ballet, *Skating-Rink*, given at the Theatre of the Champs-Elysées, with scenery and costumes by Fernand Léger. I composed the music for the *Douzième coup de minuit* ('Twelfth stroke of midnight'), poem by Carlos Larronde, for *Art and Action*, directed by Madame Autant-Lara.

For the Swiss Exhibition of 1939, the representatives of the

Canton of Neuchâtel proposed to me that I write the score for *Nicolas de Flue*, Swiss saint who had just been canonized at Rome. The poem was by Denis de Rougemont. The war prevented its performance in Zürich and the piece was given two years later at Lausanne.

William Aguet was responsible for my début on the radio, by proposing a *Christopher Columbus*, which we dedicated to Claudel and Milhaud in memory of their great work on the same subject. Later, still for Radio Lausanne, came the *Battements du Monde* ('Heartbeat of the World'), and *Saint Francis of Assisi*. Aguet had a feeling for the radiophonic theatre beyond any other; his productions always had the approval of technicians and of authors of taste.

I almost forgot a little musical accompaniment for Montherlant's *Pasiphae*. The Studio Essai requested this score from me, but it was never produced, the subject in the meantime having been judged immoral.

*

One of the greatest joys of my life has been to have Paul Claudel as 'librettist'–if, indeed, the marvellous poems of *Joan of Arc at the Stake* and *Dance of the Dead* can be called 'librettos'.

Unlike many literary figures, Paul Claudel showed great interest in whatever touched music. Perhaps musicians might find his opinions a bit disconcerting; for example, an inexplicably tender feeling for Berlioz was balanced by a solid animosity towards Wagner.

In the theatre, he knew how greatly music could contribute and how it could add value to the text. He was not interested in opera as such, or lyric drama–for he deplored this compartmentalization imposed by custom, which dictates that everything on the stage must be sung, even that which cannot be. He wanted the theatre to synthesize all the elements of a performance, each finding its appropriate place.

For each of the works in which I had the happiness of collaborating with him, he pointed out to me scene by scene, I might almost say line by line, what was the musical structure of the score. He forced me to penetrate the atmosphere, feel the density, the melodic contour, which he wanted, and which he entrusted to me to express in my own language. His precision may be measured by the directions he supplied for the last scene of the *Soulier de Satin* ('The Satin Slipper'):

1. Wind instruments (various flutes), extremely fresh and and sharp, holding the same note indefinitely to the end of the scene; from time to time, one of the instruments ceases, highlighting the adjacent instruments which continue to hold the sound;

2. Three plucked notes, in an ascending scale, on the stringed instruments;

3. A bowed note;

4. Thin roll of the drum-sticks on a small, flat drum;

5. Two small metal gongs.

6. Ventral and in the centre, an explosion on an enormous drum.

It was less easy to comply when he made a note like the following: 'The music imitates the sound of beating a carpet'; but he was serious when he suggested for the first scene of *Joan of Arc at the Stake* a colour and imagery which I did my utmost to follow to the letter:

Scene I. The voices from heaven: 'A dog is heard howling in the night. Once, twice. At the second of these, the orchestra blends in with the howling in a kind of sob or sinister laughter. At the third occurence, the chorus. Then silence. Then "the voices of the night over the forest" with which are mingled, perhaps, very feebly, the song of Trimazo and the clear impression of a nightingale. Then silence, and some bars of sorrowful meditation.

Then again the chorus, with closed mouths. *Crescendo. Diminuendo.* Then distinct voices: "Jeanne! Jeanne! Jeanne!" '

Thus the whole musical atmosphere was created and the score prescribed, so that the composer had only to submit to its guidance to realize the material sound.

It was sufficient to hear Claudel read and re-read his own text. This he did with such plastic force, if I may so put it, that the whole musical pattern emerged in relief, clear and precise, for whoever possessed a modicum of musical imagination.

*

Yes, I have had many collaborators, and almost as many joys. Young men who read me, choose your poets well, and never forget a saying much more authoritative than any of mine, that of Corneille: 'The friendship of a great man is a gift of the gods.'

CHAPTER 11

Present and Future

*

Our works have lost the two ancient
conditions for perfection: leisure for
ripening, design for endurance.
                    PAUL VALÉRY

BG. Not long ago you sponsored an inquiry, published in *Figaro*.
The theme was the evolution of musical language. You had
advised me to draw a parallel between the imperceptible evolution of literary language and the very rapid evolution of musical
language. You yourself, as was fitting, were one of the first
to respond to this inquiry. In your opinion, the matter of musical
vocabulary is secondary: the important thing, the only thing,
is the thoughts the composer seeks to express.
AH. That is still in essence my feeling today.
BG. And yet, according to some, a composer's genius will
depend on his harmonic originality.
AH. If that had been true, music would have died long ago. But
other possibilities besides the search for new materials for sound
remain.

There are two categories of composers, it seems to me. There
are those who have dared to bring new stones to the building;
and those who have shaped them, put them in place, and built
cottages or cathedrals from them. For the first, the task is

accomplished as soon as others make use of new intervals–fourths-, thirds-, tenths-of-a-whole-tone. For the others the search may continue, depending on the degree to which one has something to say. For there are no powerful new harmonies or melodic lines not already used, but there is always an original use of old or new harmonies. Personally, I believe that writer and composer are confronted with the same problems. Remember the answer by Louis Beydts in the *Figaro* inquiry: 'There is general agreement in the judgement that André Gide is the best writer of our time; yet he uses exactly the same words that Racine used.'

BG. It is none the less true that young composers also fall into two groups: those who seek the renewal of thought rather than language, and those who wish at all costs to find new words to express their thoughts.

AH. There are no new words. All the words have already been used: only new combinations remain to be found. To make myself clear, I shall remind you that the combinations possible between the twelve chromatic notes which constitute our sound resources are mathematically limited. To go from the first to the fifth step, or to return from fifth to first, implies a series of melodic contours which are of necessity reproduced. Hence it is no longer possible to invent a melody which does not recall one or the other of these contours. This fact permits the critic or any listener to state that there is nothing new in modern music.[1]

The same is true of the chords which comprise the twelve chromatic sounds superimposed. For thirty years they have been in steady use by composers. Yet, today, it is impossible to add a

---

[1] 'It must be thoroughly recognized that, with but rare exceptions, the composers of our day do not have the melodic gift; their melodies betray a painful lack of invention, of imagination, and they almost always fall back on formulas and platitudes. Our melodic insolvency appears to be an indisputable fact.' (Boris de Schloezer, *Contemporary Music*.) If Mr de Schloezer were a musician, he would avoid such superficial statements, which have been copied by Scudo, Pougin, and other subscribers. *Author's note.*

thirteenth supplementary sound: the material content is complete.
B G. What future do you assign to the researches which take
thirds, fourths, or tenths of a whole tone as a starting point?
A H. I do not in any sense believe in the success of these risky
undertakings. I repeat: the human ear is being steadily dulled,
for the quite simple reason that it is subjected to the wear and
tear of noise such as our fathers never knew.
B G. Did our fathers possess an ear more sensitive than ours?
A H. In the first place, they did not ask from music the din
that we require. Instead of noise, they preferred nuance, and
attached much value to slight variations in the quality of tone,
to which we are profoundly indifferent. The public of music
lovers was much restricted and more cultivated, capable of
following closely the unfolding of a bit of music, and of appreciat-
ing its quality. In J. S. Bach's time, a prince could propose a theme
for a fugue. Ask that today of the King of England or of Stalin!
Today we are more gourmands than gourmets. Look at the
cinema: some of the film music, composed by cheap contractors,
contains things to make you howl, so horrible is the sound
quality, so defective the harmonization, so clumsy the orchestration. You wait for a minor riot: but no, they listen, with the
same impassive ear as to a worthy score. The average listener at a
concert is responsive to the impact of the work as a whole; he
scarcely refines at all on the details, which escape him anyway.
B G. We shall become then rather like the drunkard whose
oesophagus is so burned by alcohol—
A H. That he could drink petrol without a reaction! Noise
benumbs our ears in the same way, and I truly believe that a few
years from now we shall detect no differences except between
large intervals. We shall lose sight of the semitone, and arrive at
no longer perceiving anything but the third, then the fourth,
finally the fifth. Rhythmic shock increasingly plays the pre-
dominant role and no longer the sensual delight in melody.
Think of Erik Satie's music, which some musicians look upon as

genius, and the degree to which it reverts to a primitive simplification of language—an absence of harmonic richness, an absence of contrapuntal richness. At the rate at which we are going, before the end of the century we shall have a very scanty and barbaric music, combining a rudimentary melody with brutally stressed rhythms—marvellously suited to the atrophied ears of the music lovers of the year 2000!

BG. Nevertheless, our era does follow on a period of extreme, perhaps excessive, refinement. Is ours not simply a reaction to the school of Fauré and Debussy? A brutal reaction, perhaps, but temporary? All reactions, for that matter, are temporary.

AH. It is true that around 1920 Cocteau gave the signal for music in the trenchant style—its champion was Satie and some of my colleagues of the group called *Les Six*. But well before that date, a Strauss, a Stravinsky, a Schoenberg, had rebelled against Debussyism. What Debussy had predicted for Wagner had happened to himself: 'Wagner is a sunset which is mistaken for a dawn.' That was a very apt statement, but it applies to all great innovators who open a door and close it behind them. Of course, there always arises a kind of school around any great artist. But the epigones propagate little more than the faults and obsessions of their idol.

*

BG. How do you judge our era?

AH. What strikes me in our era is the speed of change, the premature, short-lived methods. It took centuries, from Monteverdi to Schoenberg, to achieve the free arrangement of the twelve notes. Beginning with that discovery, evolution suddenly became very rapid. We are all in front of a wall: everyone seeks to find an exit through this wall, which stands before us today, made up of all the materials, piled up little by little; and each seeks it according to his individual intuition.

On the one hand are the champions of the method according to Satie, advocating the return to simplicity. *Sancta simplicitas!* On the other hand are those who forty years later revive Schoenberg's researches and seek the exit by means of atonality, by erecting even more arbitrarily the twelve-note system. This serial system prides itself on a very narrow codification; the dodecaphonists remind me of criminals who, having broken their chains, would deliberately attach balls weighing a hundred kilos to their feet in order to run faster. Their dogma is quite comparable to that of the school of counterpoint, except that the aim of counterpoint is simply to make the pen more flexible and to stimulate invention by exercise, whereas the serial principles are presented not as a means but as an end!

I believe that for a composer there is no possibility, no future, for expression there, because its melodic invention is subjected to uncompromising laws which shackle free expression of thought. I am not in the least opposed to discipline freely accepted, even sought out, by sensitive artists. But this discipline must have some justification and not be arbitrarily set up as a decree.

Again, anarchic freedom, as concerns the harmonic consequence of superimposed lines, opens the way to the most dangerous fantasies. Listen to what René Leibowitz says, the eminent theoretician of dodecaphony: 'It follows that the composer's thought can finally express itself in an entirely linear (horizontal) fashion, *since no vertical restriction can retain its hold on him.* There are no forbidden dissonances, no fixed harmonic formulas (such as the finals of modal counterpoint, or the harmonic degrees of tonal counterpoint); which is to say that the composer can give free rein to invention for his voices, which will thus gain at the same time a total individual freedom and the means of free superimposition upon one another.' And farther on: '*the immanent possibility* for the composer to write in a purely horizontal manner, without any *a priori* vertical concerns'.[1]

[1] René Leibowitz: *Introduction to Twelve-note Music. Author's note.*

Evidently, the restrictions imposed by formulating an orthodox series of notes are largely compensated for by this freedom. This explains why the young men least gifted in musical invention have enthusiastically thrown themselves on this technique. Nevertheless, it is not to be forgotten that the listener hears music vertically, and that the most complex contrapuntal combinations lose all interest and reveal nothing more than an elementary facility when they are allowed to pass beyond all discipline.

A further inconvenience in the twelve-note system is the suppression of modulation, which offers so many endlessly renewed possibilities. 'To pass from one area to another,' Leibowitz admits, 'is *vaguely* the equivalent of what is meant by modulation at the heart of tonal architecture.' Finally, I mistrust the poverty of the form, 'since one may say that each dodecaphonic piece is nothing but a series of variations on its initial series.'[1]

The aim of any conquest is to enlarge space, to abolish frontiers, not to constrict them. Creative efforts have always been in the direction of a liberation from formulas and conventions. But how many examples to the contrary all around us! Thus demagogies evolve toward an imperialism more autocratic than those they have destroyed, while dictatorships return to demagogy. I strongly fear that the twelve-note fad—we already see its decline —may initiate a reaction towards a too simplistic, too rudimentary music. The cure for having swallowed sulphuric acid will be to drink syrup. The ear, fatigued by intervals of ninths and sevenths, will welcome with pleasure accordion music and sentimental songs.

BG. At the same time, Alban Berg has found his development in the direction you condemn.

AH. Because he has not applied this serial dogma in all its rigidity. Alban Berg was not a twelve-noter, but atonal. On occasion, he permitted himself some vigorous invasions into the

---

[1] René Leibowitz: *Schoenberg and his School. Author's note.*

accursed realm of tonality, thus violating the law of the uncompromising dodecaphonist. Hence a certain suspicion around Berg: young extremists going so far as to say that he was, finally, nothing but a popular fabricator of Viennese waltzes.

BG. Nevertheless, Berg's reputation seems solidly established.

AH. Because he still represents a fine point of reference! This does not alter the fact that the best parts of *Wozzeck* are those where Berg has violated the rule. I shall cite as an example the great orchestral prelude which precedes the last scene: it is very close to being a passage which a disciple of Wagner might have written.

BG. Musical France has one fine trump card in the game: Olivier Messiaen.

AH. I have much admiration and fellow-feeling for Olivier Messiaen. He certainly stands at the head of his generation. Works like *Regards sur l'Enfant Jésus*, the *Visions de l'Amen*, the *Petites Liturgies*, and his great symphony, *Turangalilâ*, are among the most outstanding of recent years; they attest a creative temperament of undeniable power. I like his ample melodies, even when decrying their sensuality. I prefer melody, even if voluptuous, to no melody at all. I am responsive to the effort that drives Olivier Messiaen toward the large conception.

He has worked out a system and, in his *Technique of my Musical Language*, a textbook, he explains with laudable candour the methods he employs—less shrewd than the prestidigitators who obstinately refuse to give up the secrets of their tricks.

What is more, this system is very clear, and easily detected, especially in his later works. But it is evident that it no longer aids its author; on the contrary, it weighs on his shoulders. That, alas, is fatal!

Two or three years ago some journal set up an inquiry. It asked some twenty contemporary composers if Messiaen showed genius. This reminds me of a conference some thirty years ago at the Salle Gaveau, for which a group of notables had been assembled to reply to the same question publicly, about a young composer whom I knew intimately. One defender of the young man was soundly rated by the critics because he cited Beethoven as an example. Another was charitably advised to go and spend a ten-year period under a palm-tree.

Messiaen's methods of composition, however, are very precise. We know his predilection for cascades of superimposed chords of perfect fourths and augmented fourths. Nor are we unaware of his taste for rhythmic complication and the use of church modes linked with exotic modes.

Personally, I myself remain strongly sceptical of whatever has to do with these rhythmic subtleties. They have no importance except on paper, and they remain unnoticed in performance.

I shall cite a personal example. Messiaen came to play for me his *Vingt Regards sur l'Enfant Jésus* ('Twenty Reflections on the Child Jesus') while I was having my portrait painted. I held my pose, which greatly hampered the liveliness of my responses. Present was an excellent musician of Messiaen's generation, Alfred Désenclos. One of the pieces appeared perfectly clear and luminous to me. 'How clear and limpid it is!' I exclaimed. At which Désenclos, who was following along with the score, retorted, 'I find it very complicated.' 'You are joking!' I replied. 'Here,' said Désenclos, 'look for yourself.' And, indeed, I saw that what I was attributing to a rhythmic licence was actually care-fully notated. These points, these half-units of value, lent an extreme complication to the text. The eye was dismayed, while the ear had perceived simply a passage in triple time, played with a certain *rubato*.

B G . I believe, like you, that the scientific notation of a *rubato* is fanciful. It adds up to giving oneself a lot of trouble for nothing, for a sensitive interpreter would of his own accord retard or accelerate this or that passage.

A H . The same thing happens in music particularly rich in con-stant changes in time signature. After a rehearsal of the finale of Stravinsky's *Symphony in Three Movements* the musicians in the orchestra were all saying something like: 'We did not have time to listen and judge: we were counting the quavers all the time!' This preoccupation with the metronome takes away all freedom from the author and the interpreter.

BG. What do you think of the mystical literature with which Messiaen clothes his music?

AH. It may have some influence on certain listeners. I myself admire his wealth of imagery, but I do not always comprehend its significance. However, we have no right to transfer to the music itself the effect, negative or positive, produced by such unbridled literary associations.

BG. Messiaen, who is paradox become man, characterized himself in a significant chapter title in his *Treatise*: 'The Charm of Impossibilities'. This is his way of claiming to combine theology and sensual pleasure: all because he has borrowed certain paroxysmal utterances from sacred writings.

AH. The confusion was tempting. *The Song of Songs* is a sacred book; it is also a love poem. The way in which St. John of the Cross describes the mystic trance demonstrates that it is very close to sensuous ectasy. I believe that certain men experience the sensuality of asceticism, or, if you prefer, that asceticism for them becomes a kind of sensuous pleasure.

BG. Otherwise there would be no more ascetics.

AH. Basically, all that is of small importance. Messiaen shows the instincts of a true musician, and therein lies the value of his work.

*

BG. Furthermore, Messiaen is not the only composer of his generation. There are Duruflé, Dutilleux, Gallois-Montbrun, Lesur, Jolivet, Baudrier, Landowski, Jean Françaix, Rivier–

AH. In one small book built around the profession of composer, we can hardly enumerate the many musicians of the generation that follows ours, much less analyse their works. I am very happy, however, to recognize the brusque harshness of André Jolivet, which does not preclude tenderness; the genuine dramatic and symphonic power demonstrated by Marcel Landowski in his *Jean de la Peur* and *Le Rire de Nils Haverius*. Duruflé's beautiful *Requiem* has merited the suffrage of all musicians, as well as of the public. Gallois-Montbrun, Lesur, Baudrier are composers of much talent and thoroughly versed in their profession. Jean Rivier, author of a remarkable *Psalm*, has written five symphonies of an arresting quality. Finally, quite objectively I appreciate the subtle art of a Jean Françaix, even though it is quite remote from my own preoccupations. Many others might be cited!

I do not wish to linger over my own contemporaries: Milhaud, Auric, Poulenc, Tailleferre, Ibert, Delvincourt, Louis Beydts, Marcel Delannoy. They are too well known for it to be necessary to assign them a reputation already won. Others, despite great talent, have not yet the reputation they deserve—such as Harsanyï, Mihalovici, Hoérée, and others still whom I do not name. The number of talented artists is greater than ever, and, unfortunately, their opportunity to be heard by the general public is deplorably restricted.

BG. Have you heard of *musique concrète*—those symphonies of human or inhuman noises, sometimes made by a person's mouth, sometimes by the bottom of a saucepan?

AH. Let's not call it a discovery. These montages of sounds arose from some tentative experiments in 1912 by the school of Italian *bruitistes*, noise-makers, Russolo and Marinetti. Such experiments are legitimate and do not irritate me. Why not bring order into the noises of forges, aeroplane motors, as we make use of the sounds of a violin, a flute or a trombone? Some excellent results might be produced, profitable for cinema or stage music. But is it not another proof of what I was arguing above? We have to excite the senses, strike on ear-drums ever more atrophied. We are no longer at the era when Rossini, for a few thumps on the big bass drum, could be hailed as 'Il Signor Vacarmi!'

BG. Have you not been struck by the obsession which overtakes so many young composers to make a clean sweep of all that precedes them? To be totally original or not to be–that, for them, is the question.

AH. It is a childish ambition, but a very natural one, though never appeased. It would be nice to create out of nothing, that is, without the participation of anyone else, not even those who lie sleeping beneath the earth and are no longer dangerous rivals.

The surprise effect of a discovery is soon dissipated, and behind the greatest innovators one quickly discovers the masters who inspired them: Wagner behind Schoenberg, Rimsky behind Stravinsky, Saint-Saëns behind Ravel, etc.

'There is no spontaneous generation in art,' someone has said. This seems accurate to me. A long chain binds old traditionalists to the hardiest innovators: the latter loudly cry up their disdain for old-timers so as to hide under a little dust the shackles that bruise their own ankles.

*

BG. Take it all in all, your view of the music of your own time is rather sombre.

AH. Because I feel very strongly that we are at the end of a civilization. Decadence lies in wait for us, has a grip on us already. Our arts are on the way out, they withdraw ever farther from us. I fear that music will be the first to depart. The more I move about, the more I see music abandoning its calling: magic, incantation, that seriousness which must encompass all artistic manifestations. It is not the fault of musicians, but of musical life, which is being transformed. Once upon a time the concert was a means of celebration, a gathering whereby its magic was made manifest before men assembled as for a religious ceremony.

Read once more what Stravinsky most aptly said in his *Poetics of Music*: 'The propagation of music, whatever the means, is in itself an excellent thing; but when it is spread abroad without caution, and offered without rhyme or reason to the great public, unprepared to hear it, this public is exposed to the most dangerous saturation.

'The time is long past when Johann Sebastian Bach cheerfully undertook a lengthy journey on foot to hear Buxtehude. Today the radio brings music into the home at every hour of the day and night. The listener is relieved of every effort except that of turning a button. Now, musical taste can neither be acquired nor developed without exercise. In music as in everything else, inactivity leads to ossification, the atrophy of the faculties. Heard thus, music becomes a kind of tranquillizer; far from stimulating the mind, it paralyses and brutalizes it. The consequence is that the very undertaking which aimed at encouraging a love of music by diffusing it more and more, often results in a loss of appetite, even in those in whom it intended to arouse interest and develop taste.'

In 1919, Satie advocated 'music as a part of the furniture' – a music to be played without being heard, like wallpaper. Today we have brought the Mass in B Minor or Beethoven's Quartet, Op. 132, down to this level. Concerts are more frequent than ever. But they have turned into performances by champions of the piano or the baton. The impresario insists on the orthodox programme: a Beethoven festival for the conductor, a Chopin recital for the pianist. The public rushes to the box office without even knowing what the programme will be. As I said before, it is not the music that counts, but the virtuosity of execution. We live in an age when a little girl of six is placed before an orchestra so that she may gape in astonishment at its confusing activity.

People ask why so many great masters of the past wrote so many works, since they never stir the curiosity of performers. Even more reason to ask, why should so many young unknowns have the presumption to enter the lists already filled to overflowing?

And that's the curse–the word is not too strong–that weighs upon 'our profession'. Music is dying not of anaemia, but of plethora. There is too much production, too many offerings for too little demand. Apart from the French composers or those living in Paris, other countries show men of great talent (genius we reserve for the dead), such as Hindemith, Prokofiev, Malipiero, Dallapiccola, Hartmann, Toch, Egk, Orff, Britten, Walton, Absil, Frank Martin, Beck, Nabokov, Barber, Copland, Shostakovitch–and many more besides, ignored by the orchestras. Let us accept the proofs of a clear state of lethargy.

Let me be well understood: it is not for myself that I am fearful. It is for those who are entering on this career, every day more difficult of entry, more dominated by routine.

The end of our musical civilization, which can precede only by a little the end of our whole civilization, we must have the courage to envisage with clarity, as one awaits death. To deny it would be nothing more than a lack of clear-sightedness. Rebellion against it is useless. We must record it coolly. Thereafter, it is permissible to console ourselves by thinking that out of the debris of this civilization, another will be born.

Young composers, do not see in me the old fossil quite willing to leave you behind on earth, on the condition that he may poison your stay on it in advance. Persuade yourselves only that the 'profession of composer' can yield very little in the way of material means. If your works are appreciated by a few friends or contemporaries, that must suffice as your recompense and your interior joy–that is the only privilege which cannot be stolen from the creator.

CHAPTER 12

Letter to Arthur Honegger
Optimism and Truths

*

'Behold the light'
Song of Songs

Mon cher Maître,

Here then, congealed on paper, are our conversations, which were so alive and, to my joy, so extended. The transcription is faithful, the document is authentic; and, in re-reading it for the twentieth time, I discover in it no trace of that cunning which impels so many great artists to organize their own glorious legend in this world below, and then to solicit from their biographers certain slight and opportune alterations in the truth, because they think it contrary to their interests or painful to their pride. What you are you have entrusted to me; and what you have said, you have countersigned. I, who know and love you, find you in the pages of this little book, without make-up and without retouching.

The more reason, then to be concerned about the ironic pessimism of your utterances. I am amazed—and the public will be more amazed—to hear an illustrious composer, deservedly at the height of his fame, utter such bitter words, and describe

his triumphant career as a warning. I know this is your profound
conviction, and not subconscious vanity. When you systematically
discourage your students from following you in the path in which
you have been so successful, you sincerely experience a thousand
misgivings. Not for a moment are you secretly reflecting:
'Young man, if you had my talent, I should be less categorical.
But, since you do not possess it, I prefer to turn you aside from a
path without issue.' On the contrary, you give your serious
consideration to the work of others, you respect dedication;
and I have never heard you treat any effort, however hazardous,
with anything but measured judgements, marked by a considered
leniency. You are one of the rare musicians whom I have seen
rejoice at a success and sorrow at a set-back to a colleague, even
a rival. Our best colleagues, for that matter, are our greatest
rivals.

Why, then, such gloom around an inspiring subject? Why these
moody confessions, these disillusioned confidences, these ill-
omened predictions? You quite simply predict the end of music
and the explosion of the globe–the latter, indeed, involving the
former. What grounds have you for this sombre mood? Do you
expect to make your readers believe that you have plunged
within to the source of your disillusionments, and that, fêted,
cherished, celebrated, as one of the most important composers
of our times, you value the rewards of such efforts as meagre
indeed? Nonsense! We have only to see you laugh, boisterously,
as you can do, to know that you are without a shadow of those
rancours which carve their indelible grimaces on so many faces.
The critics have been quite generally favourable, the public
acclaims you, you love music with all your soul, you have
magnificently served its cause: what reason, then, will you give
your most faithful friends for a language which can only pain
them? Are you not afraid of disappointing them by presenting
such a sombre face?

You have a hundred times opened your mind to me in the

silence of your studio. Shall I admit it? You have not convinced me.

I am not sure you know the truth yourself. I do know it. I am going to tell you what it is!

*

In July of 1950 we concluded the recording of a series of radio 'Interviews'. When we touched the subject of your future projects, you confided to me, in a melancholy tone, 'I have none. I shall doubtless never compose again, feeling no need, and seeing not the slightest necessity, for it. What is the use?' These despondent words I accepted with reservations.

I met you again after the holidays. On my first visit, I noticed on the whitewood desk which serves you as a writing table a rather bulky manuscript. I asked about it.

'Is that a former work?'

'No,' you replied with a charming embarrassment, 'it's a–a little something I have just finished.'

'Ah!'

'I am given to a painful insomnia. To drive away my darker moods, I jot them down on paper. That gave me some sketches. Having put some of them together, I noted that it would make a symphony; so, I orchestrated it.'

'A symphony! That would be your number five!'

'My *Fifth*, as a matter of fact. Heaven grant that it be played as often as the other *Fifth*, if the symphonic organizations permit.'

'And this, on the piano?'

'Oh, it's nothing, a *Suite Archaïque*, commissioned by the music society of Louisville, in America.'

'Is it recent?'

'I finished it last month–one has to pass the time.'

O miracle of the human spirit, always ready to despair, but so prompt to rebound! Secretly, I bless the happy reversal which restored your waggish humour along with the creative vein.

Not talent, not even genius, are unalterable rivers. They have their flood times, they pass through their periods of low water. Beethoven and Wagner knew the lean as well as the fat cows, and I am convinced that a momentary interruption of their beloved work plunged them into a state bordering on prostration. I am even more sure that the letters of the one, the notebooks of conversations with the other, bear witness to the despondency which lies in wait for the artist between two periods of creative effort. God alone delights in rest on the seventh day after a week of creative labour; for man, to see 'that it was good' is not enough to let him taste a blessed relaxation. More demanding than the eternal Father, he is reassured only as he creates without respite: less wise than the vegetable, he wants to flower in all seasons. His nature pushes him to action as a consolation for his sombre thoughts. The man who creates awakens joyful chimes to accompany his life. 'The man who listens hears the knell,' said Léon Daudet. For an artist, to pause is to hear.

There, cher Maître, you have the explanation of your sadness. I have no doubt that if our interviews had taken place at the time you were composing *King David* with euphoric speed, the results would have been highly optimistic. You would have been too happy in announcing the end of your work to predict the end of the world. Perhaps, then, you would have painted the profession of composer in more seductive colours for your juniors.

Equally certain, you would nonetheless have expressed the most explicit reservations about an activity which, born of the impulse of the creator and seeking to arouse the appetite of the listener, rests, indeed, on the exacting demands of the spirit, more fragile than material necessities. It is a hard profession, strewn with hazards, fertile in disappointments, less assured than commerce or industry, offering its practitioners uncertain successes, and breeding more trouble than income for them.

All this is accurate enough, and you were right to draw the reader's attention to it: musicians will approve; the layman will be astonished to learn that the composing of music is a rose guarded by very real thorns.

But the rose is there! Even if it rarely shows itself between the pages of this little book, every artist will meet it on the path which it perfumes. Alongside the harsh labours, there are the moments of grace. After the tempest the port is won. To compensate for the 'perspiration' described by Saint-Saëns there is the 'inspiration' extolled by Pierre Louÿs: 'We must strain at the plough and put our foot to the spade if the tree of beauty is to flourish and give up its eternal fruits.'

Your modesty and your temperament have prevented you from uttering these fancy phrases. You have even forced those that struggled to my own lips to return to my throat. Even more, you eliminated such words of your own on the proofs which I submitted to you, assuming, no doubt, that they were of such a nature as to bring a smile to your former colleagues–for one must devote a great deal of time and care to persuade one's comrades to forgive the crime of having succeeded better than they!

Thus you have spoken only with the greatest objectivity of your difficult and wonderful profession, revealing the darker days, but remaining silent on the hours with the stars. Nevertheless, I have so often observed you laughing and unbending, not proud of what you have just composed, but content to follow your chosen life, happy to have aroused an echo in the hearts of humankind. That is the glory of the artist–and his happiness!

*

When I wished to extract from you a confidence which you thought inopportune, or simply note down a spontaneous avowal, you stopped me: 'No, no, my friend, believe me, that would be absurd!'

And I obeyed. After all, this book is your work and you speak in it the language which suits you. I confine myself to giving you simply this reply: yours is a modest role, and I am enchanted by it.

Must you give it too great an importance? You have trimmed me down, interposing in the midst of our dialogues two or three monologues, in the course of which you released the floodtide of your mood, to which I was unable to oppose the dike of my protests!

With a tiny malicious smile at the corner of your lips, you said–and I recall it well–'In the form of a preface, I shall write a letter to you. I shall compose it myself, without any help.' And then, when you observed that I was somewhat taken aback, you added, 'You may write me one as a postscript, if you wish.'

If I wish! I should think so!

Now I speak for myself. It is my turn to adopt the tone I think suitable to me.

You undoubtedly thought: 'All will have been said by the end of the volume. I can well grant him the innocent pleasure of a conclusion? What can he add?'

Good heavens, many things! For example:

A profession is worth no more than the talent which practises it. This book takes its value from the fact that it is signed Arthur Honegger, that is to say, one of the most important composers of our time. For in truth, cher Maître, you have given us much, and you will still give us many of the beautiful works you carry within you. Your music is generous and noble. Above all, it is great. Yes, you have seen on the grand scale–which in itself is very fine–and you have realized on the grand scale–which is better still. You have demonstrated that one can be young without rejecting one's ancestors, can be moving without falling into banality. You are at once original and sincere. So many of your works, your pages, make us feel that pang at the heart which only the touch of absolute beauty can supply. Again–even though a famous man—you are not intimidating. You know how to be serious when necessary, and how to smile when that is appropriate. If I had to apply one motto to you, do you know what I should select? 'Neither angel nor beast.' Because you have your feet on the earth and, sometimes, your head in the stars. Neither angel nor beast—yes, that suits you well. Amid all the false angels of music, who play the beast unwittingly, it is comforting to observe in the first rank of contemporary artists a man like others—a man who, quite simply, has sometimes the wings and the smile of an angel.

BERNARD GAVOTY

Index

*